Eizo Nishio

Sculptures & Drawings 2017-2019

Photographs by Eizo Nishio

Art & Books

Contents

Sculpture

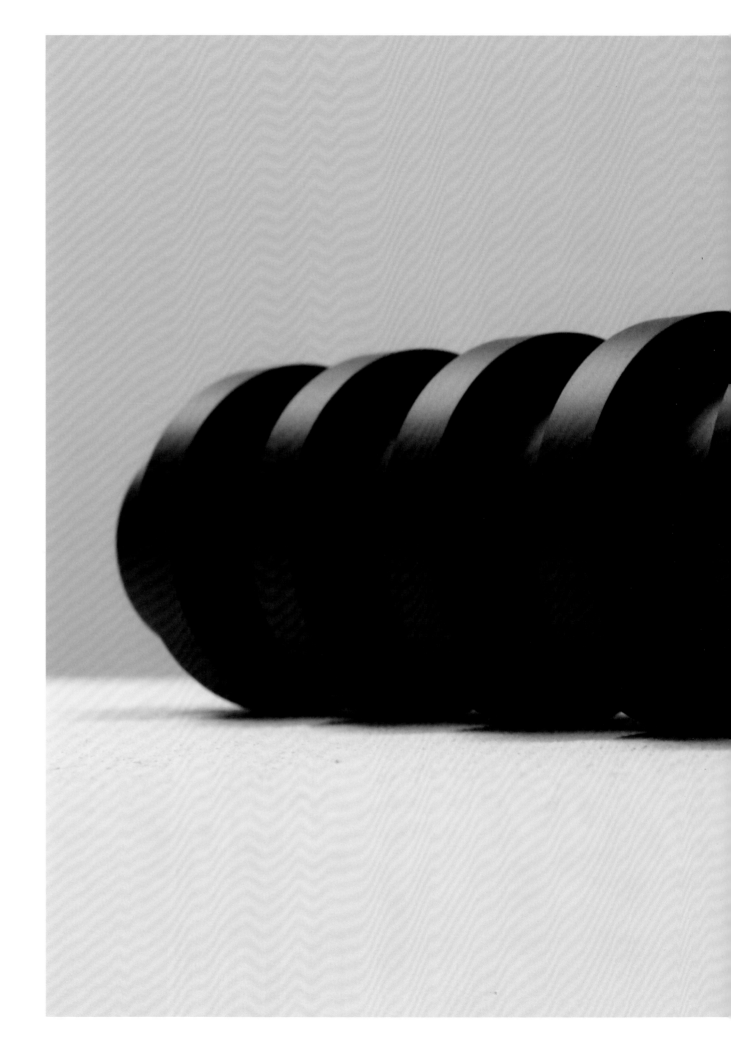

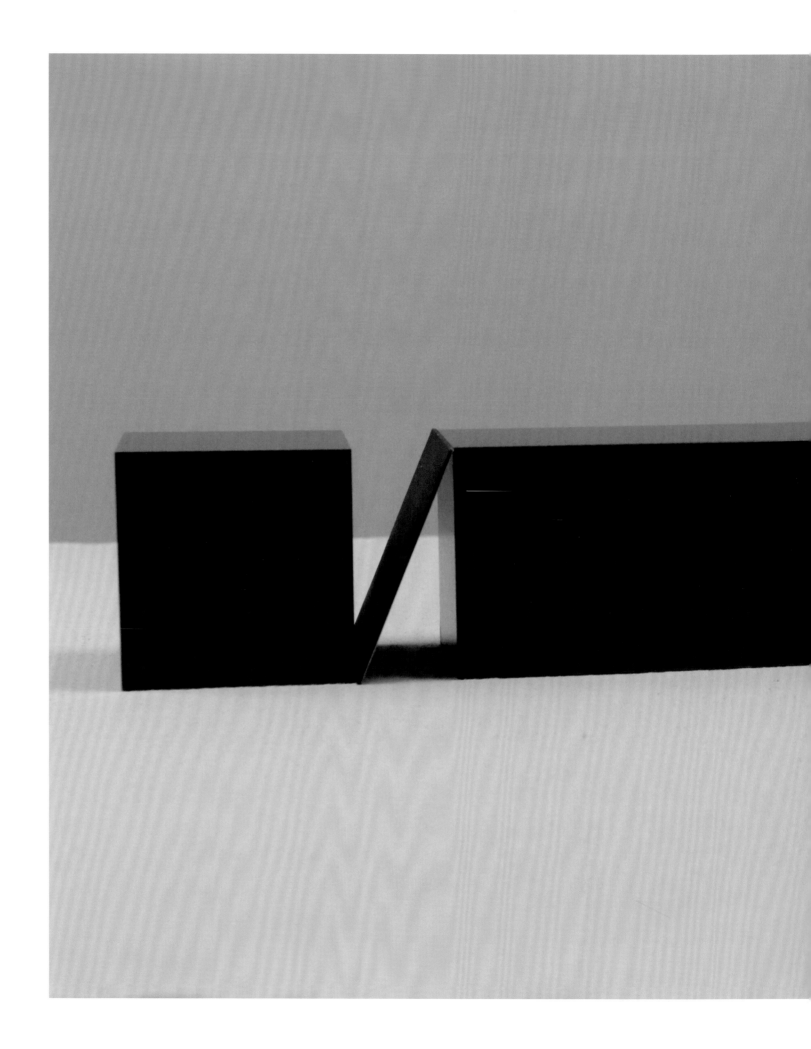

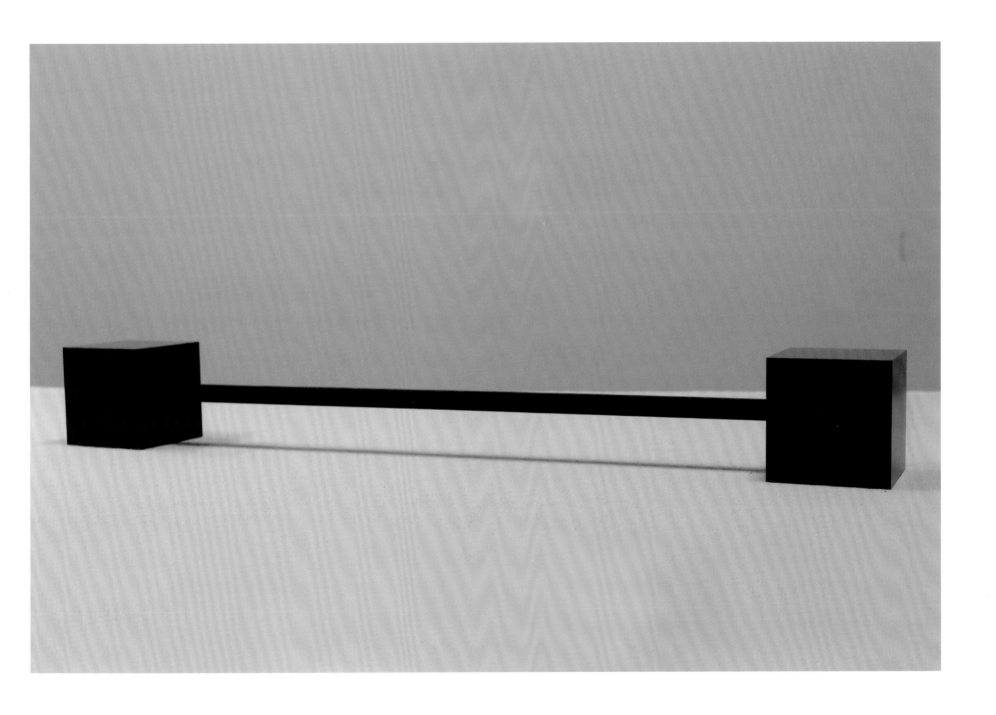

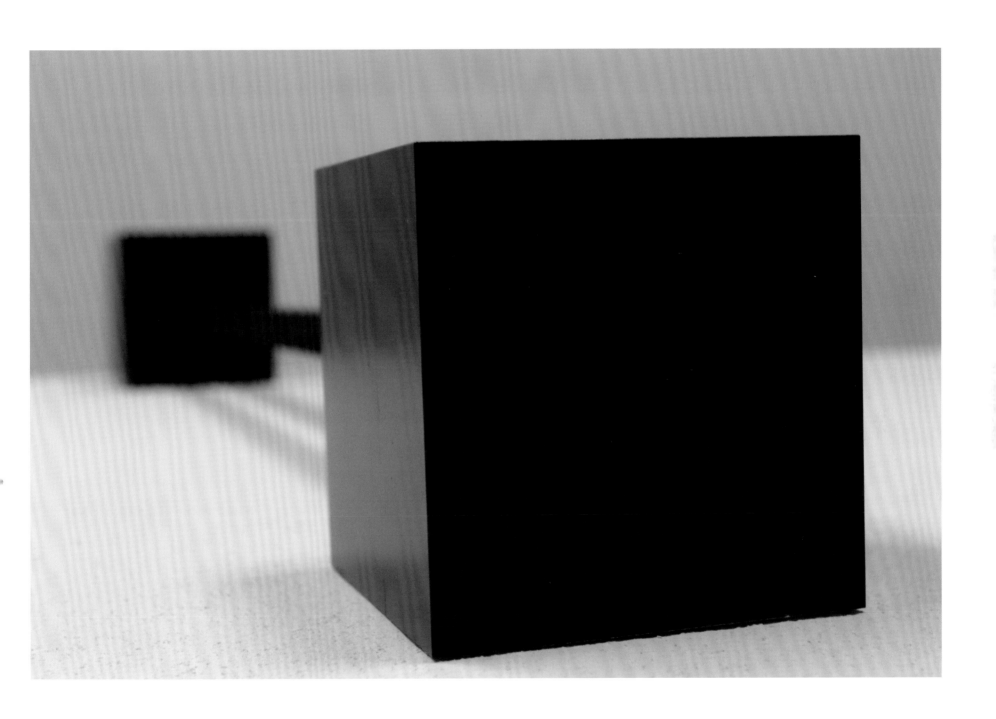

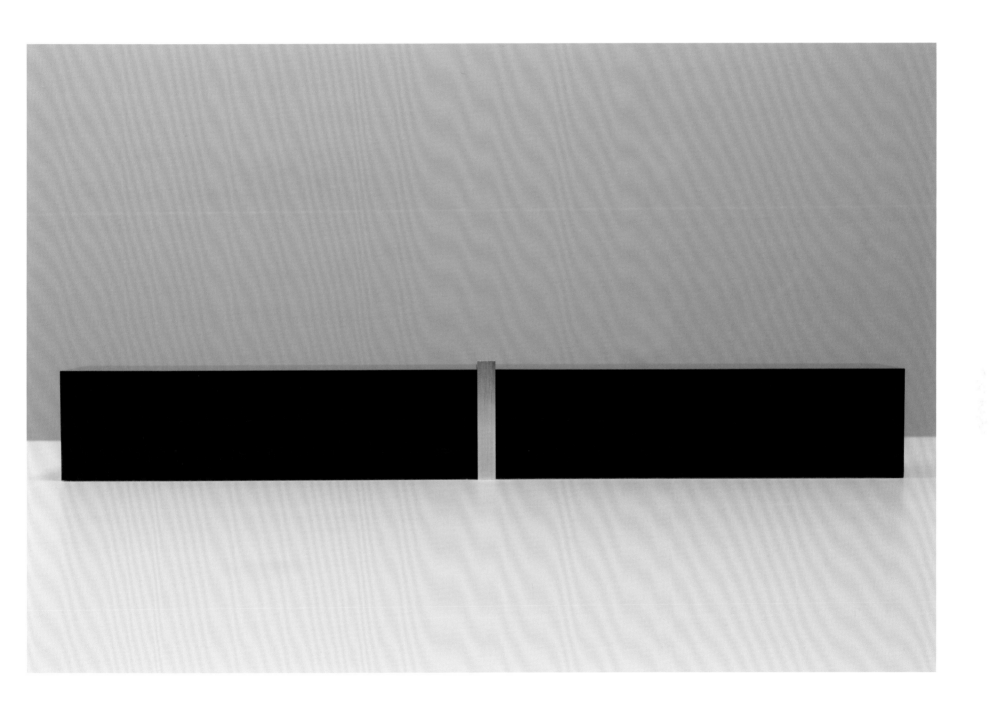

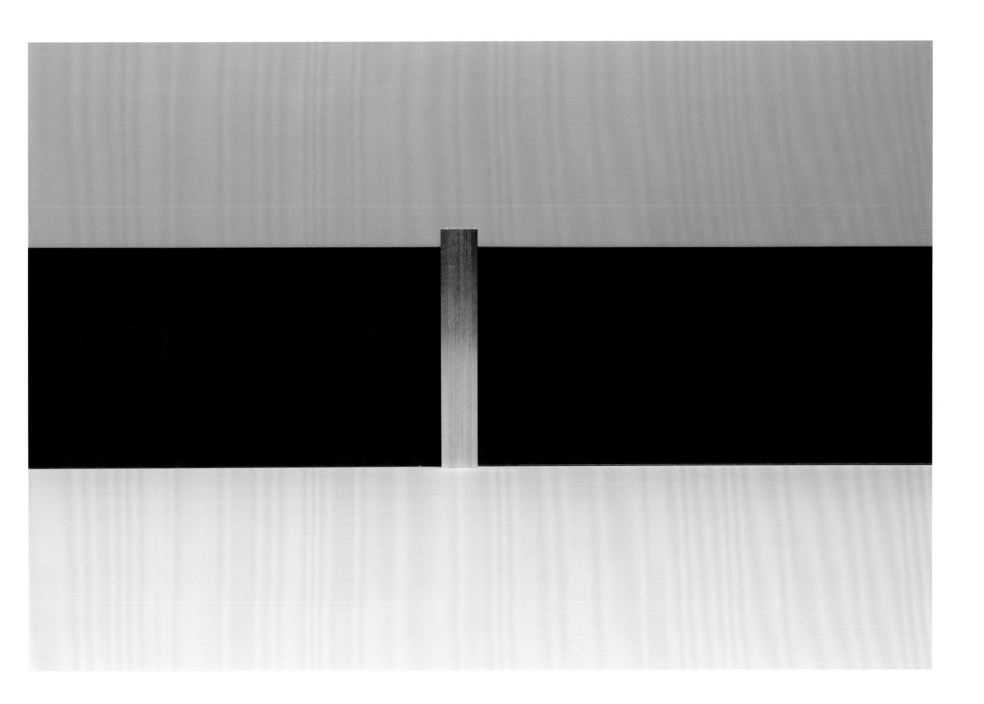

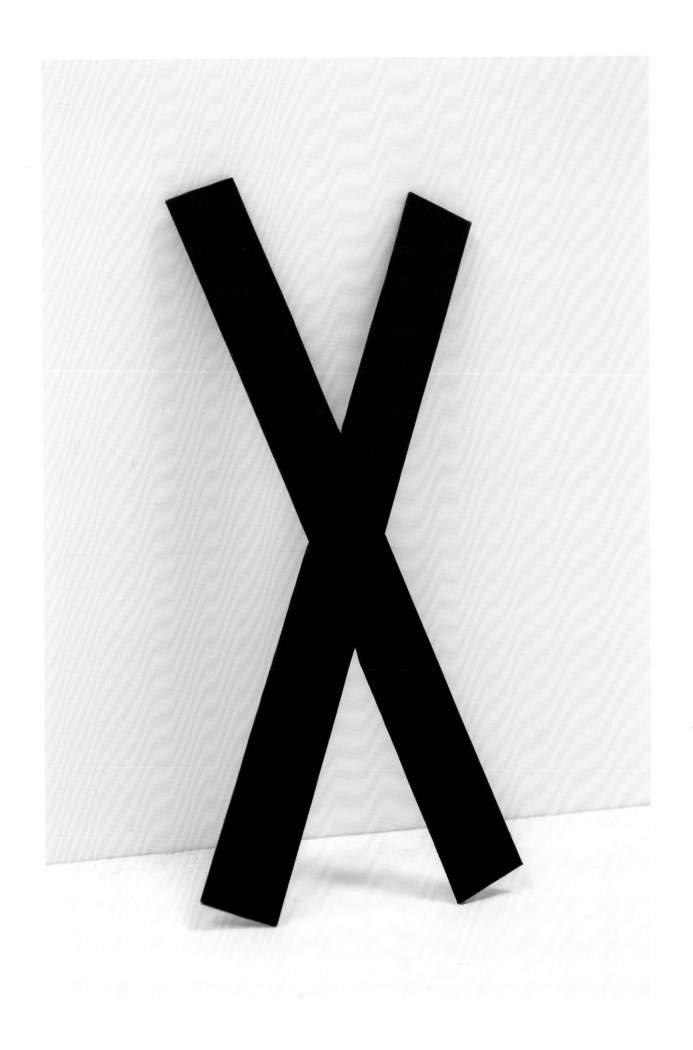

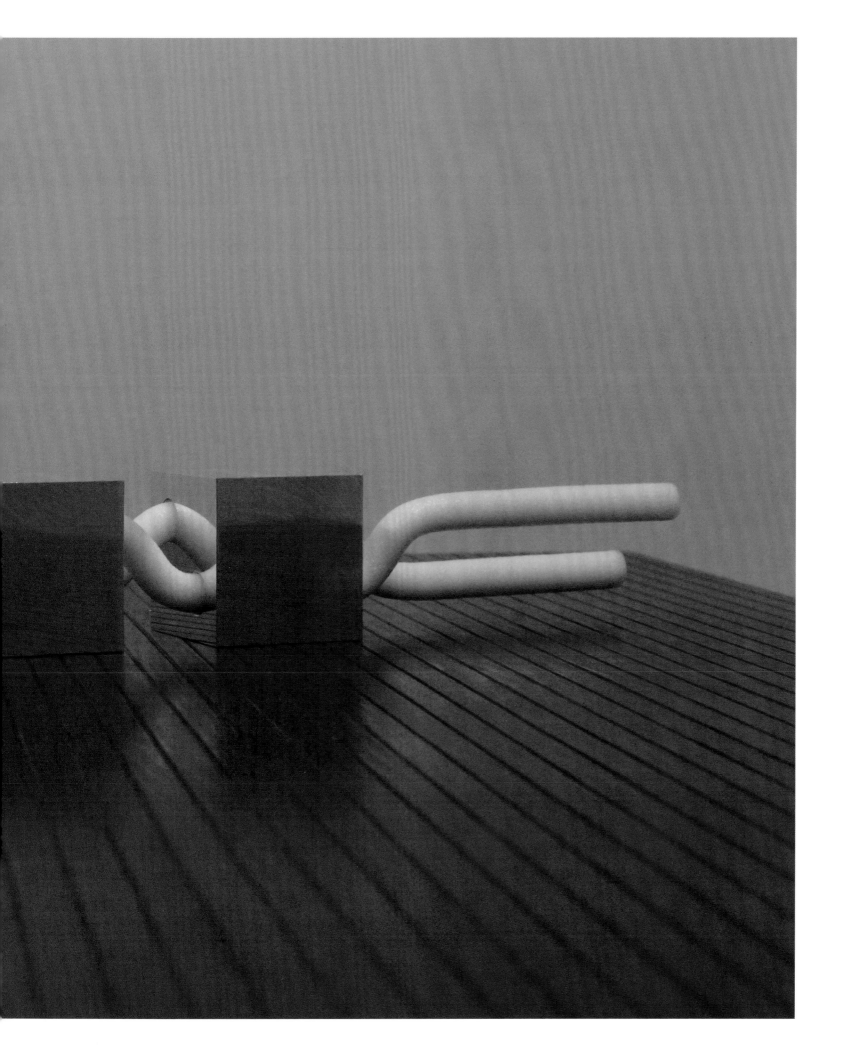

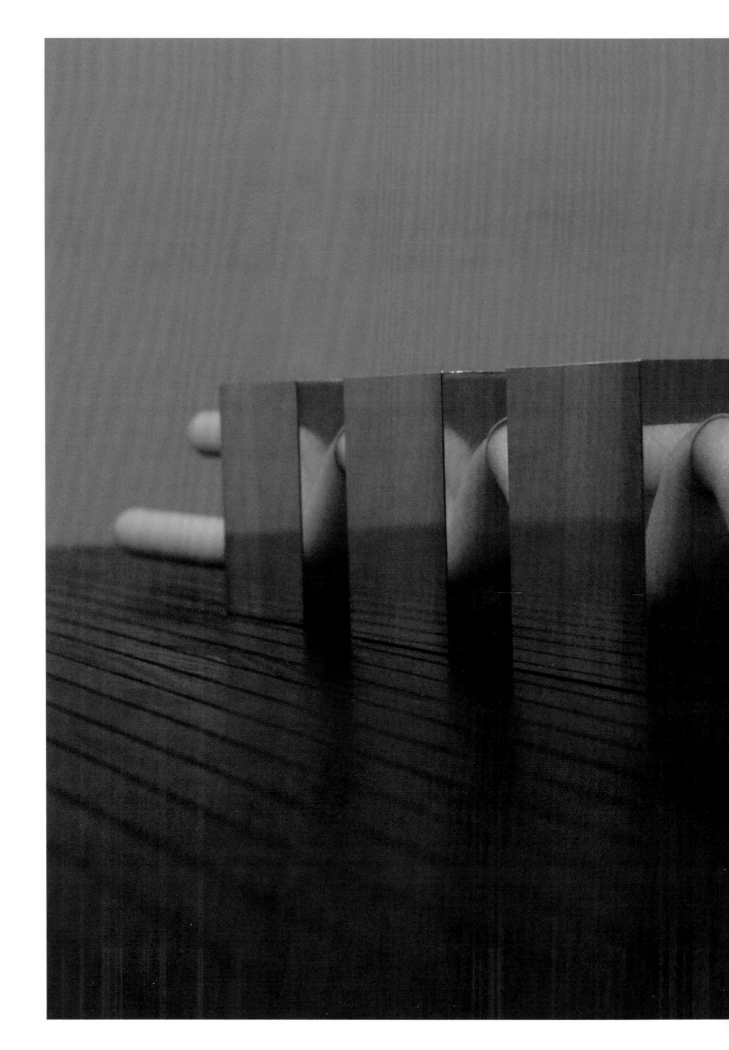

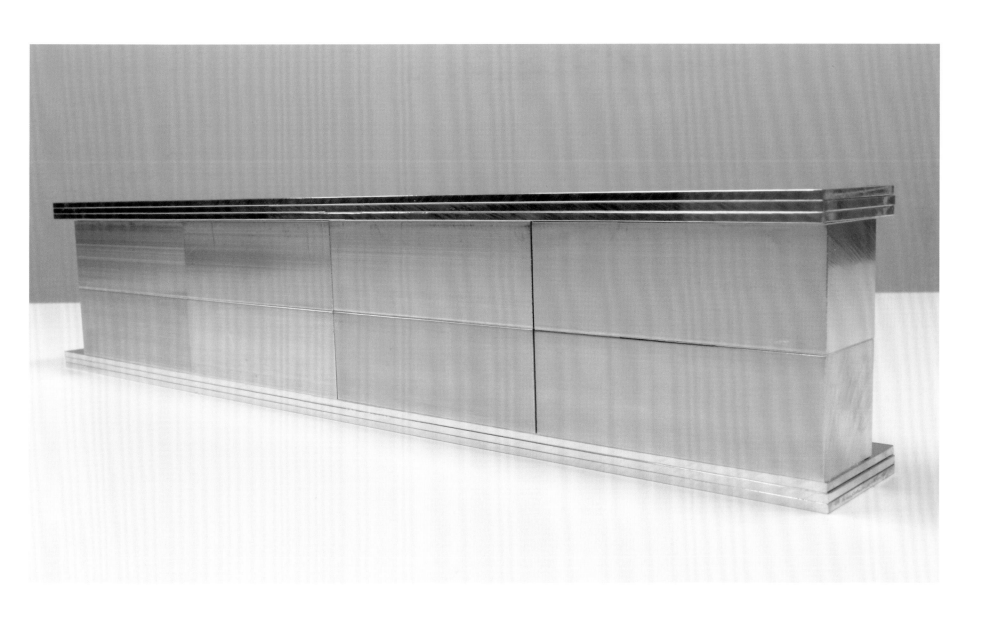

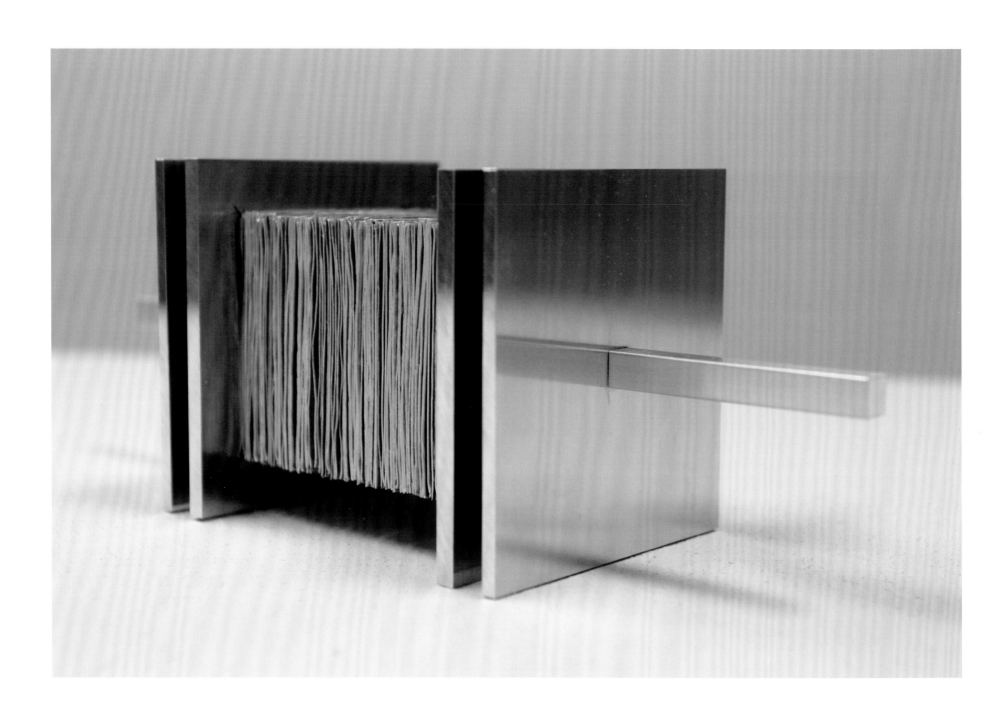

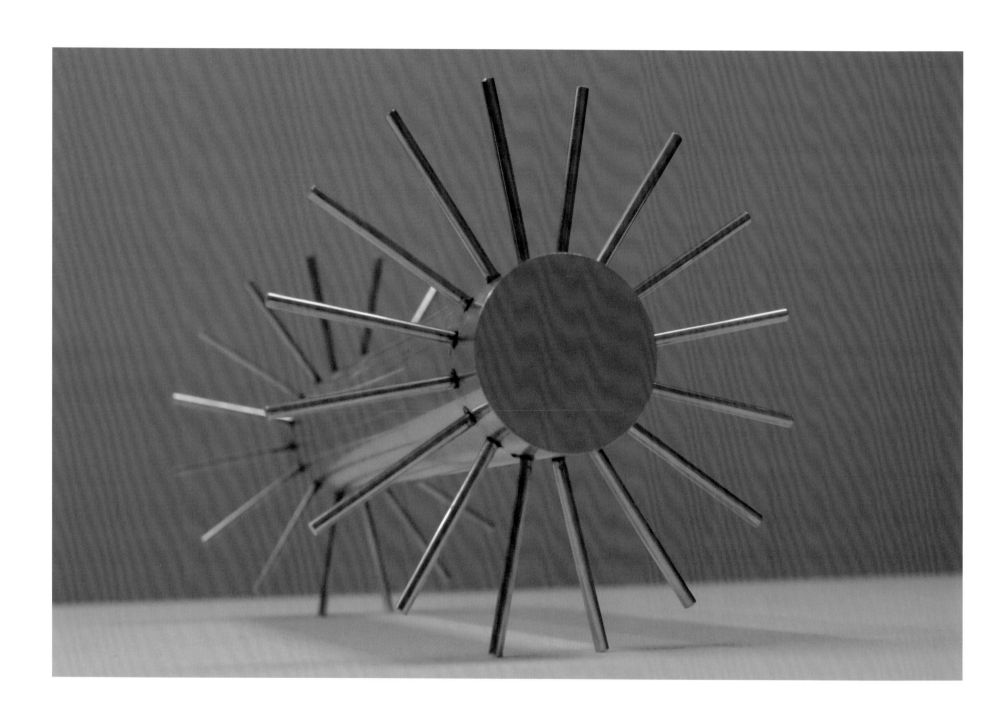

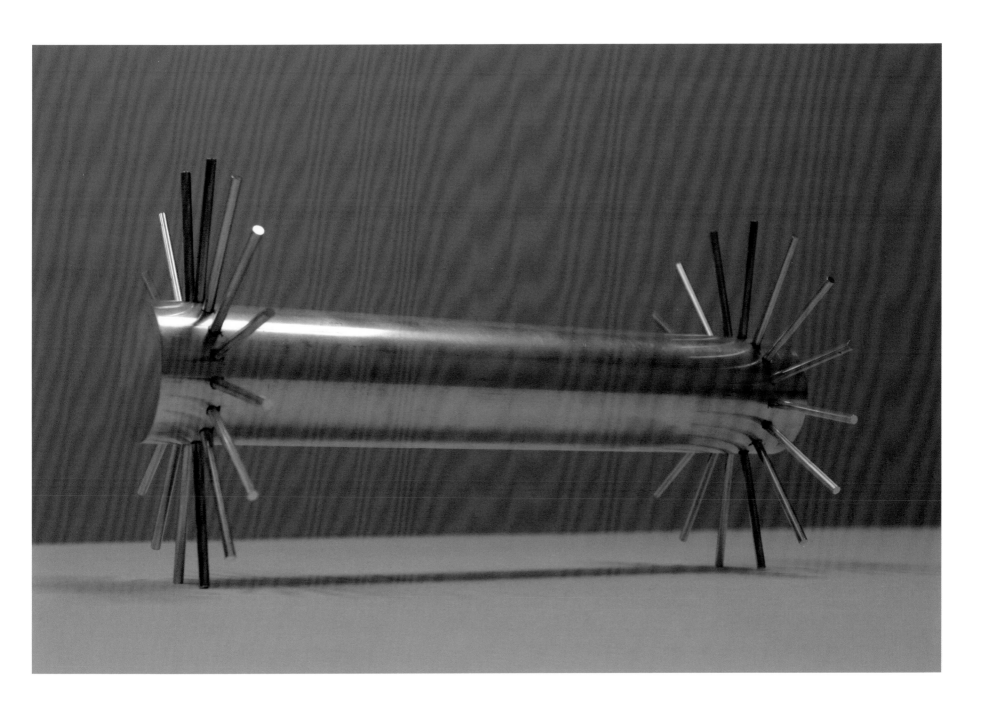

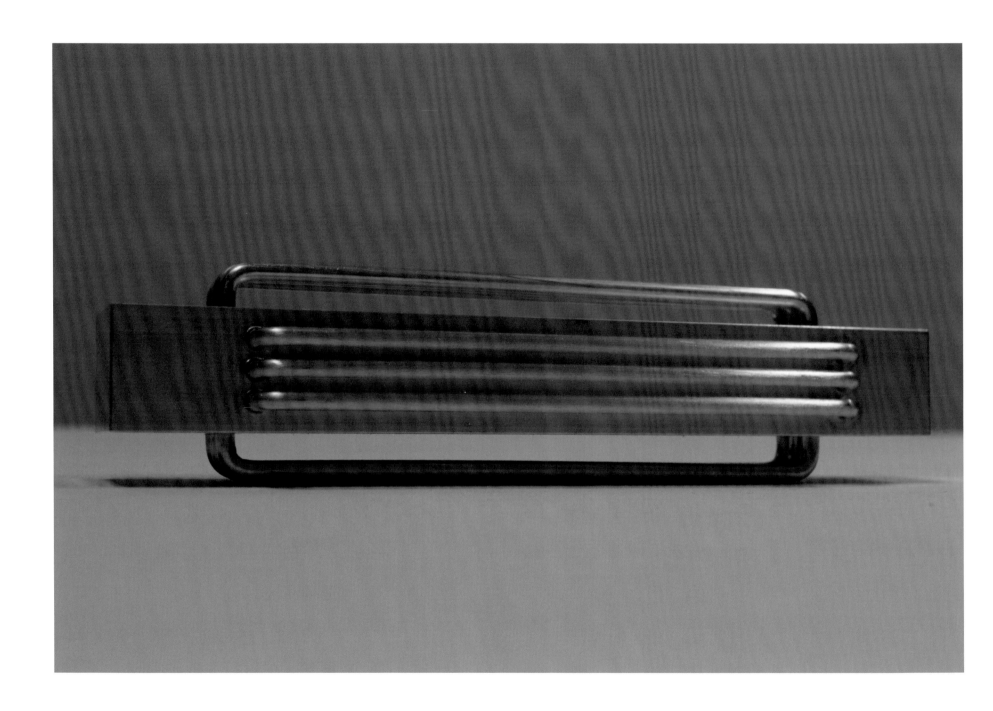

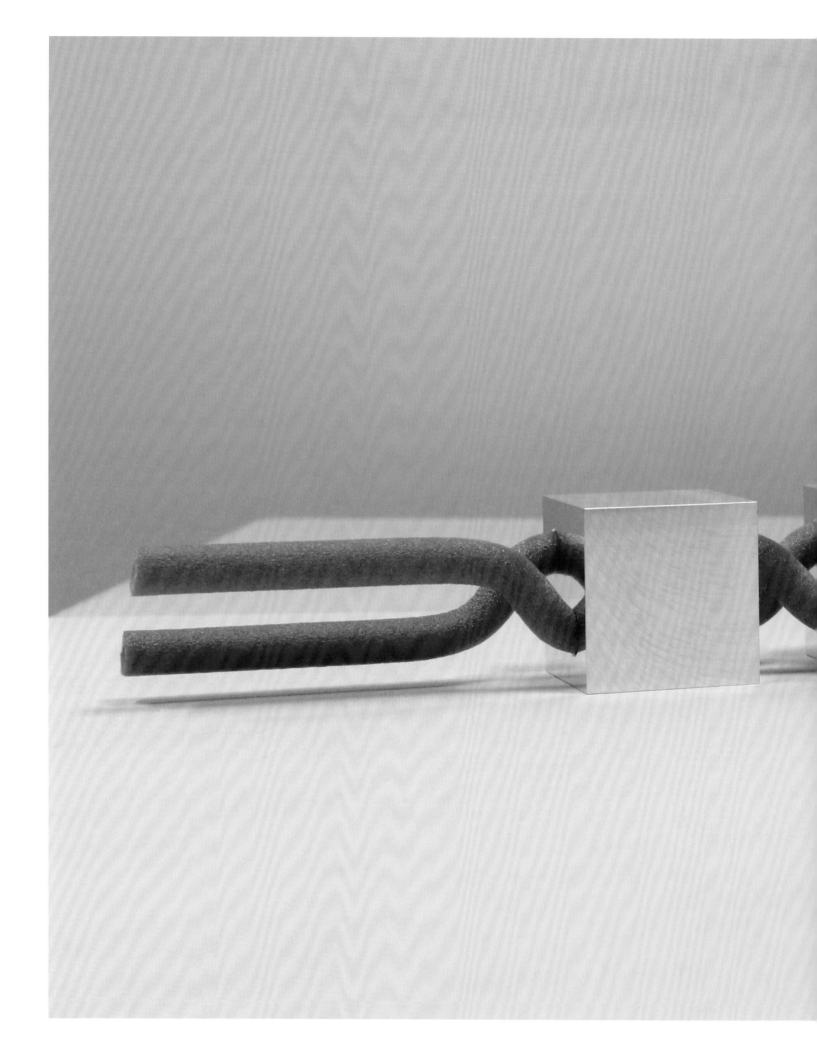

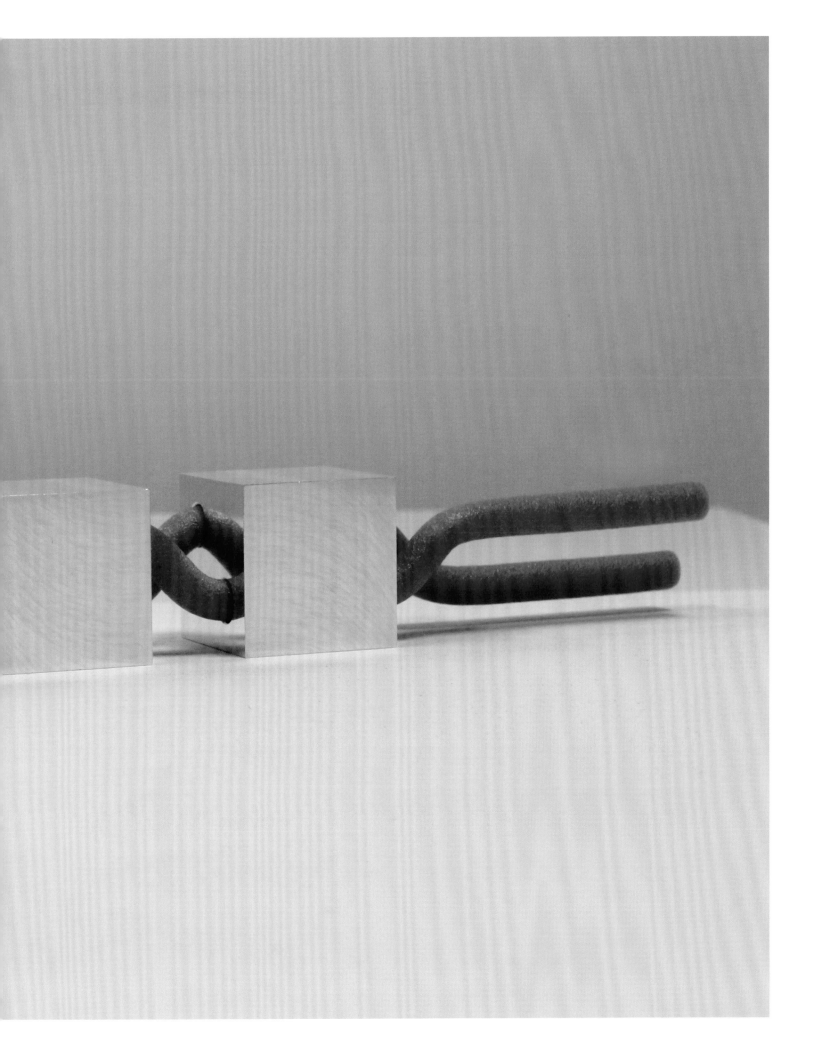

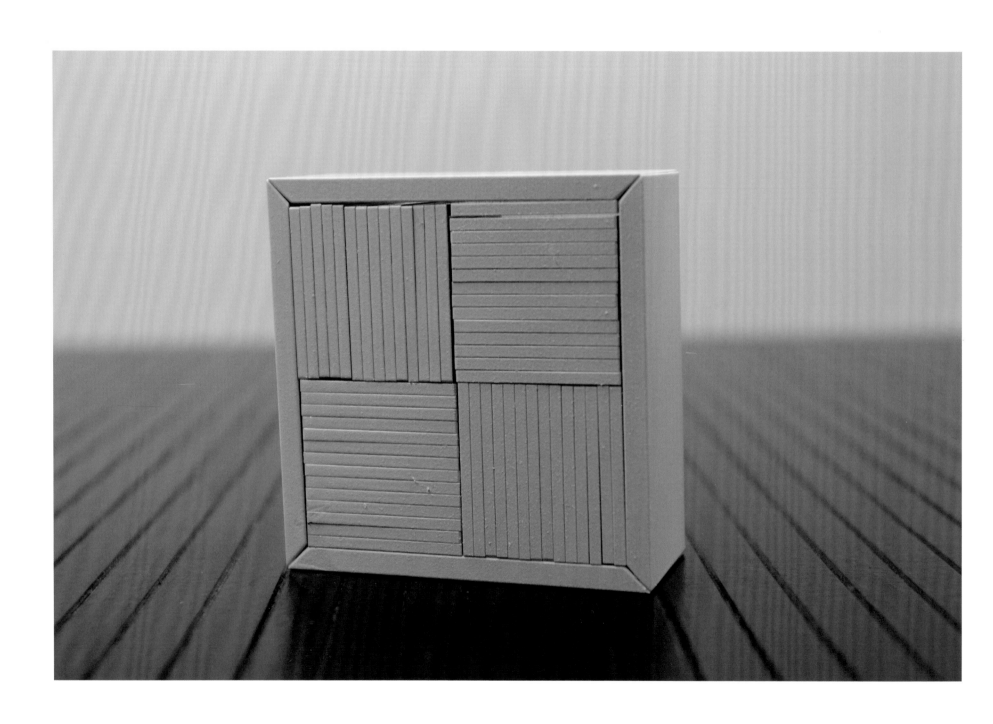

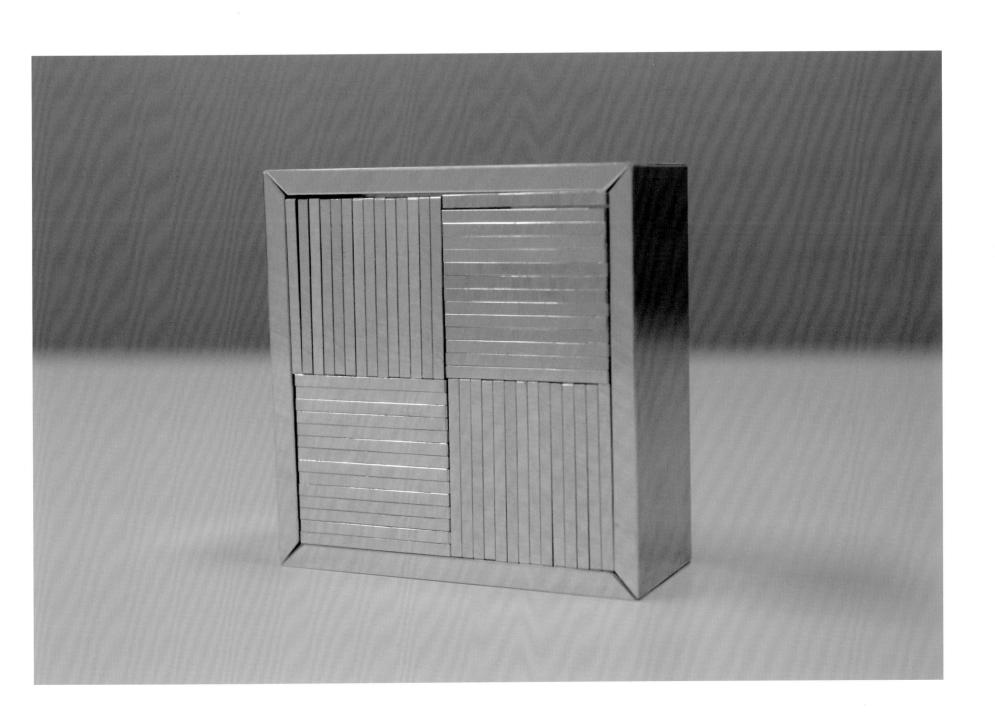

Drawing

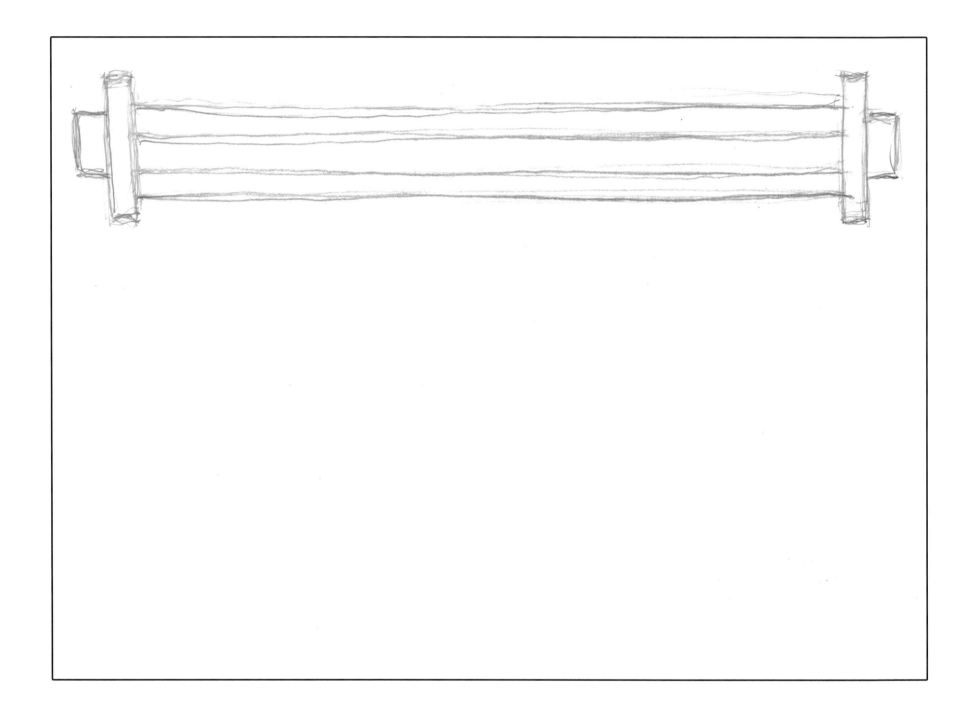

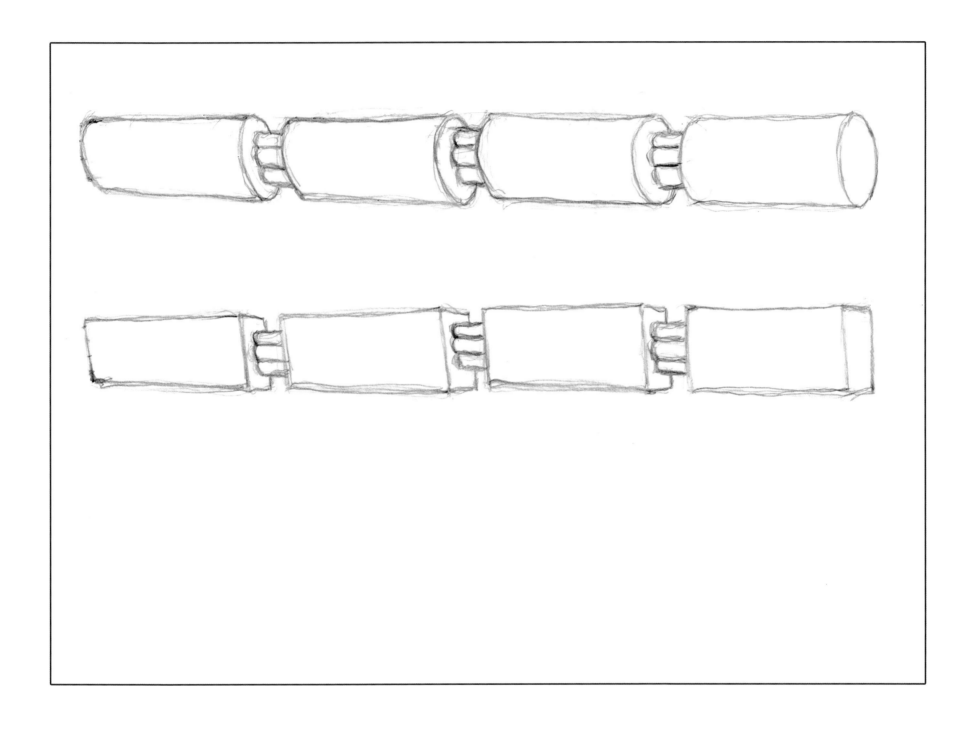

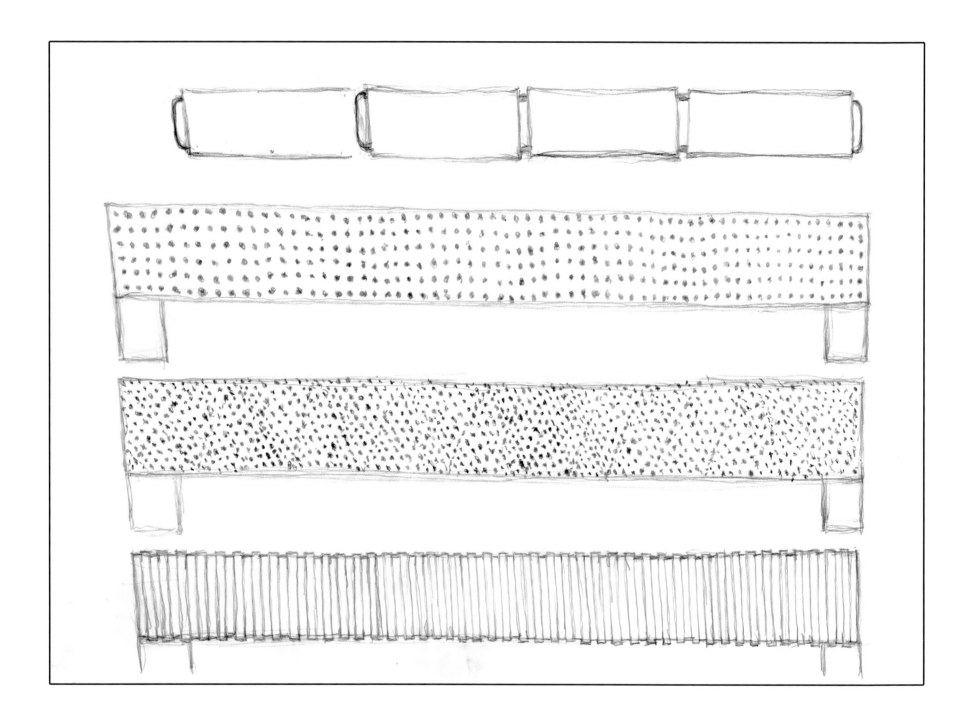

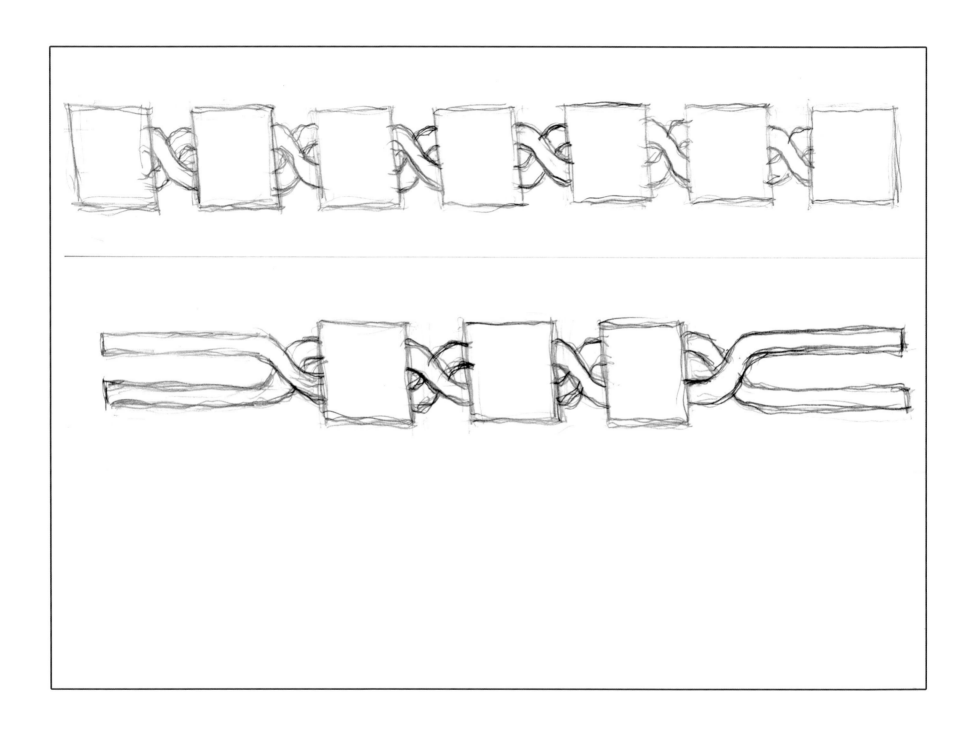

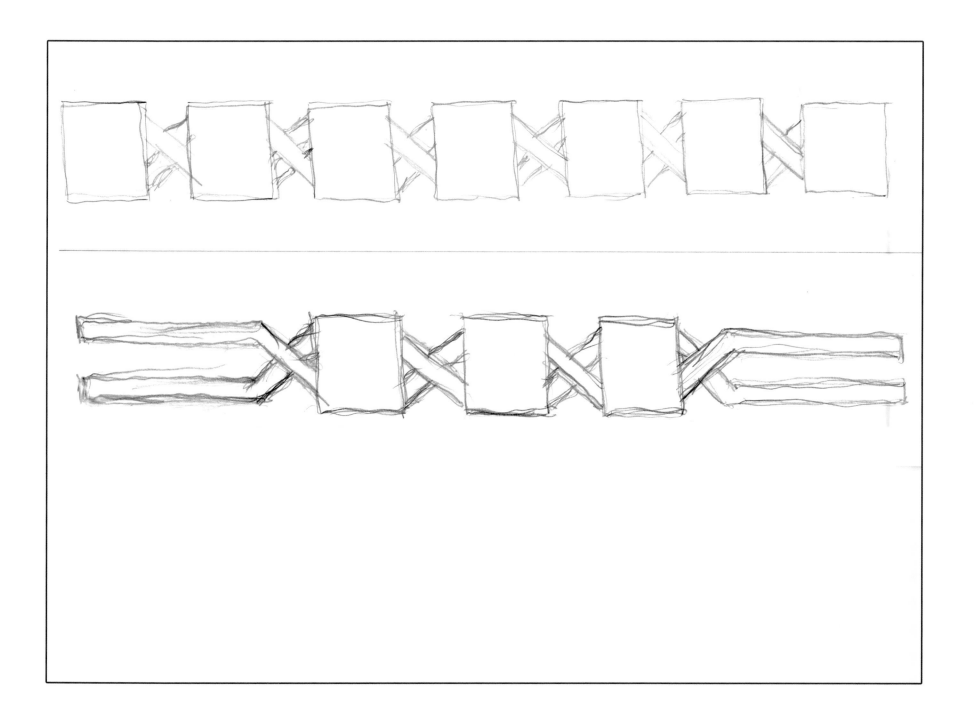

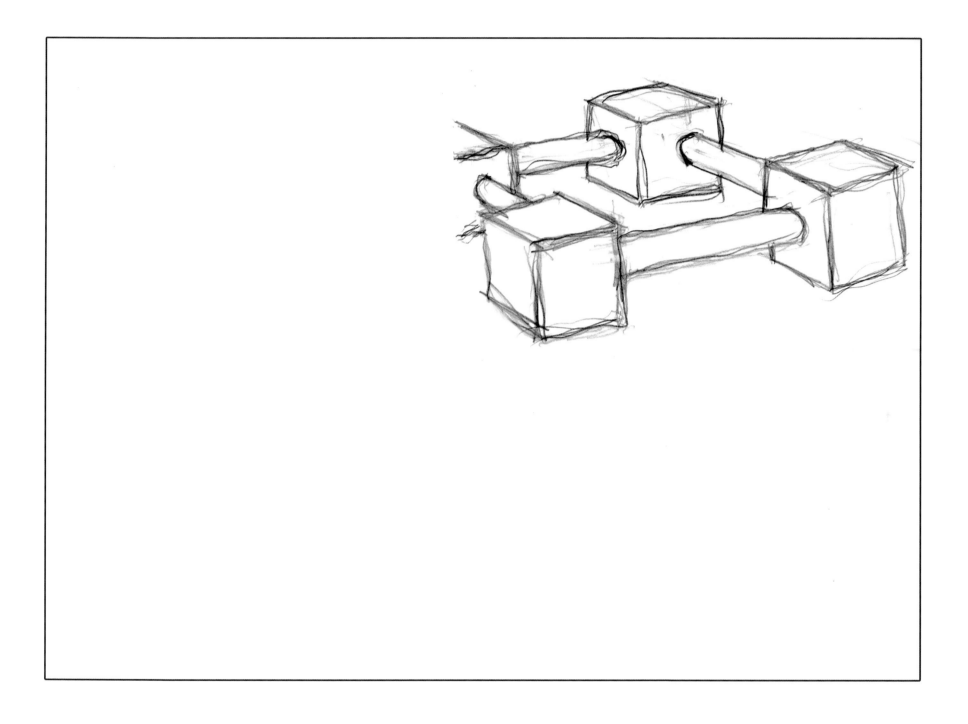

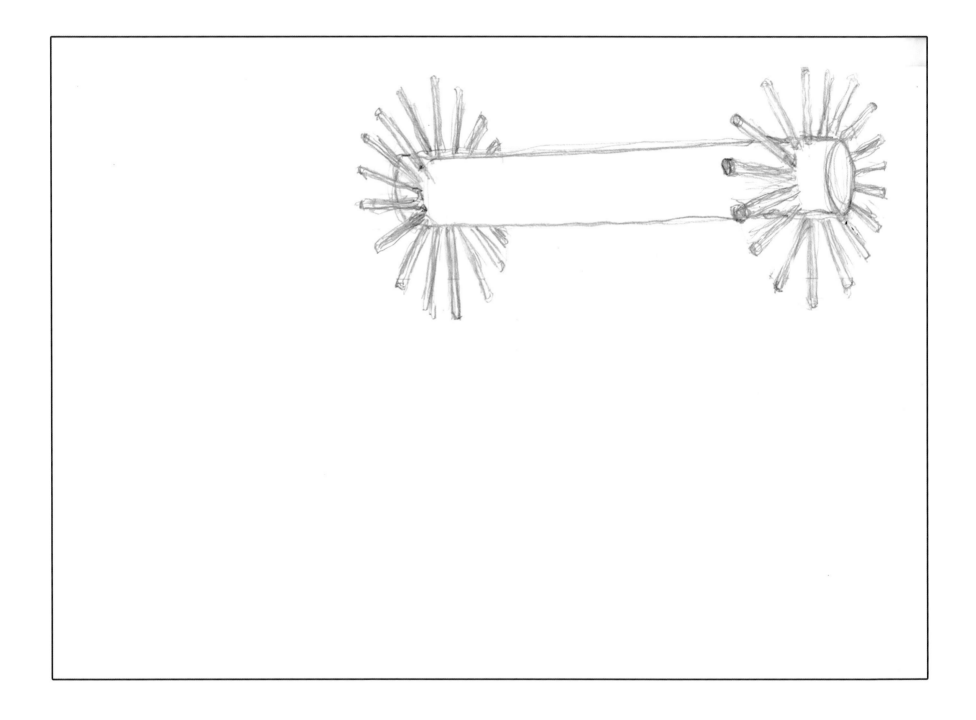

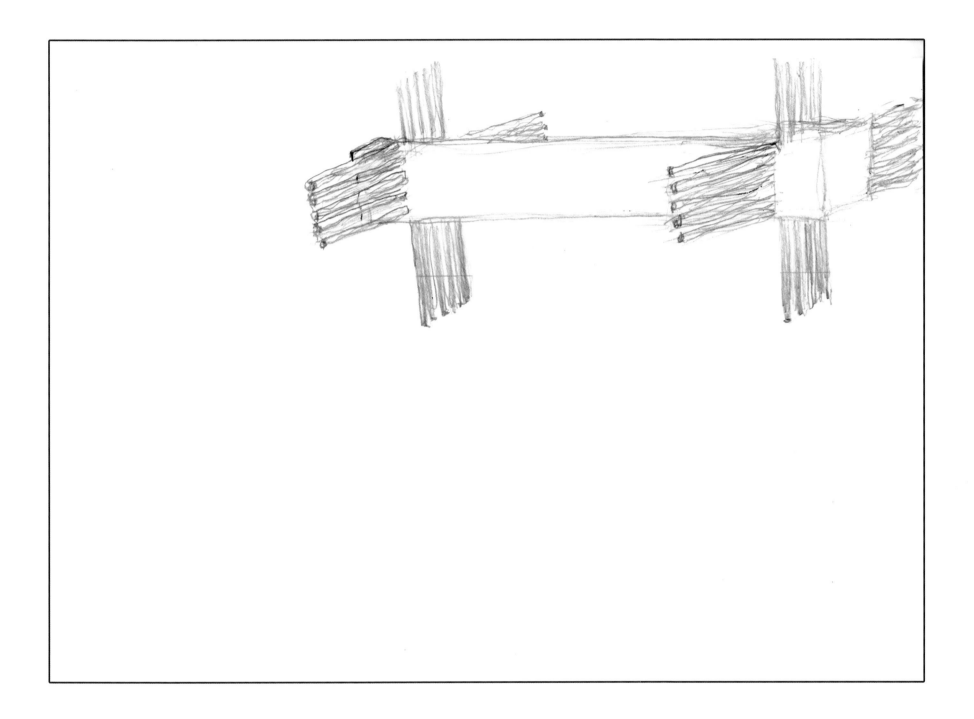

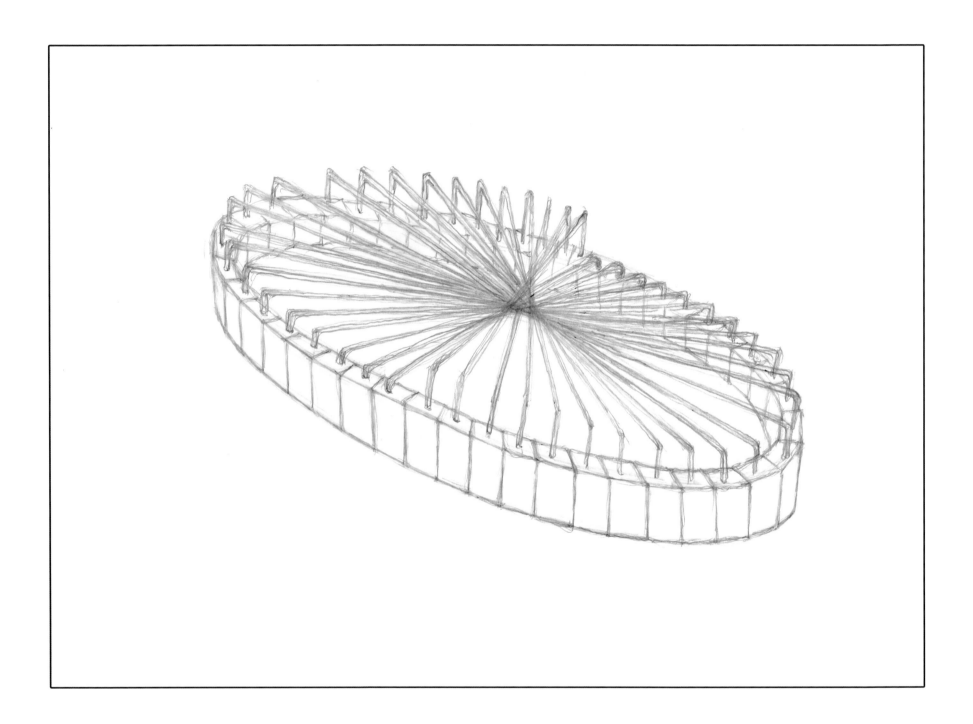

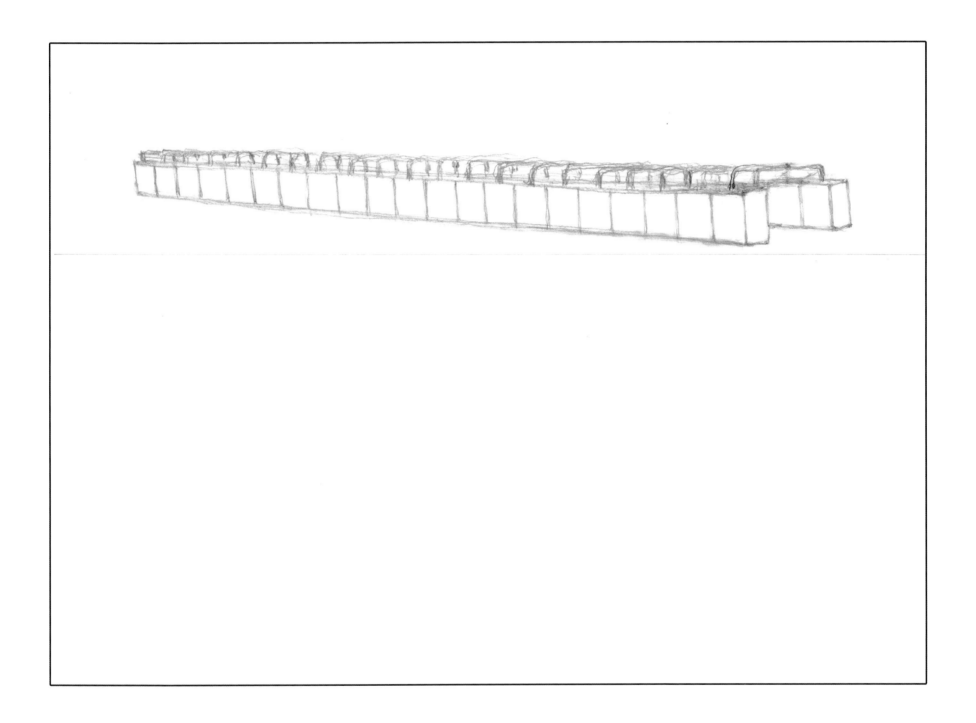

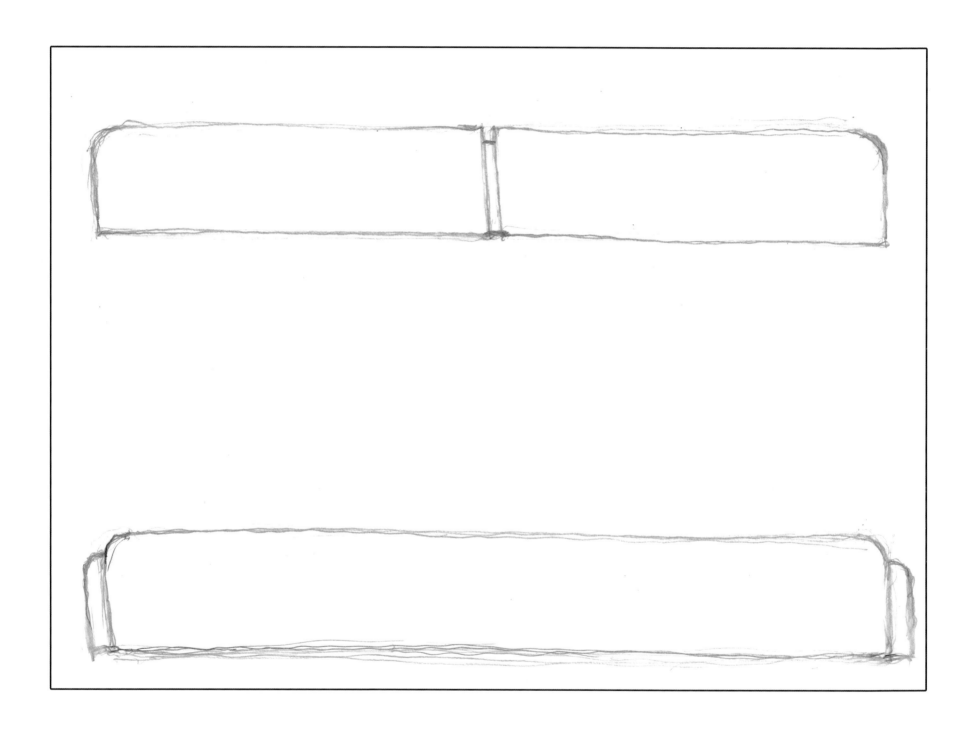

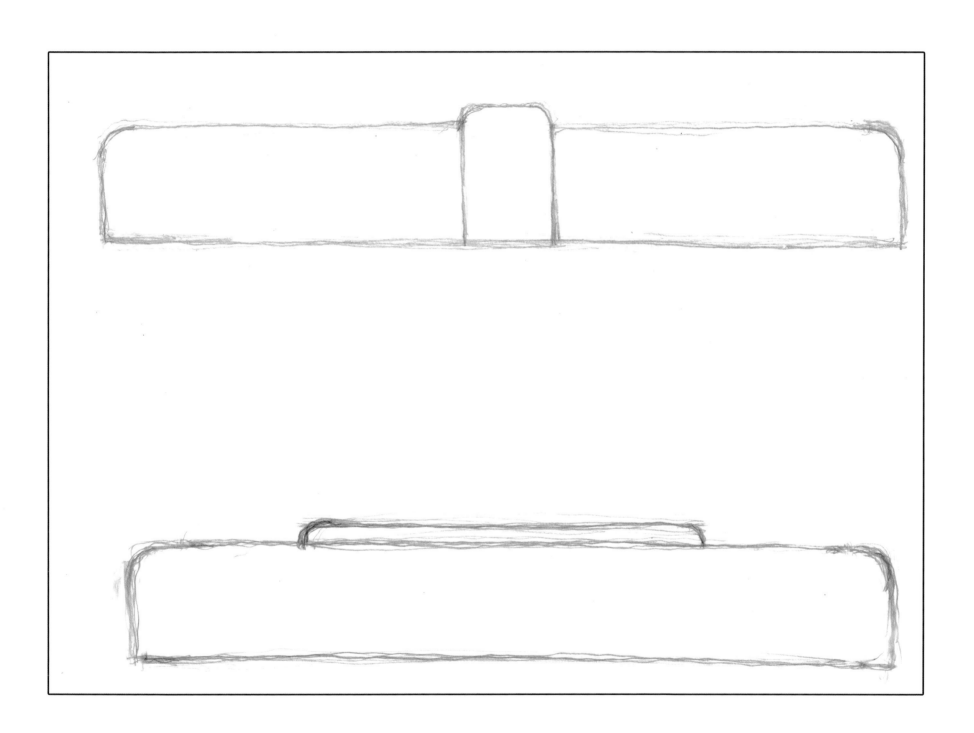

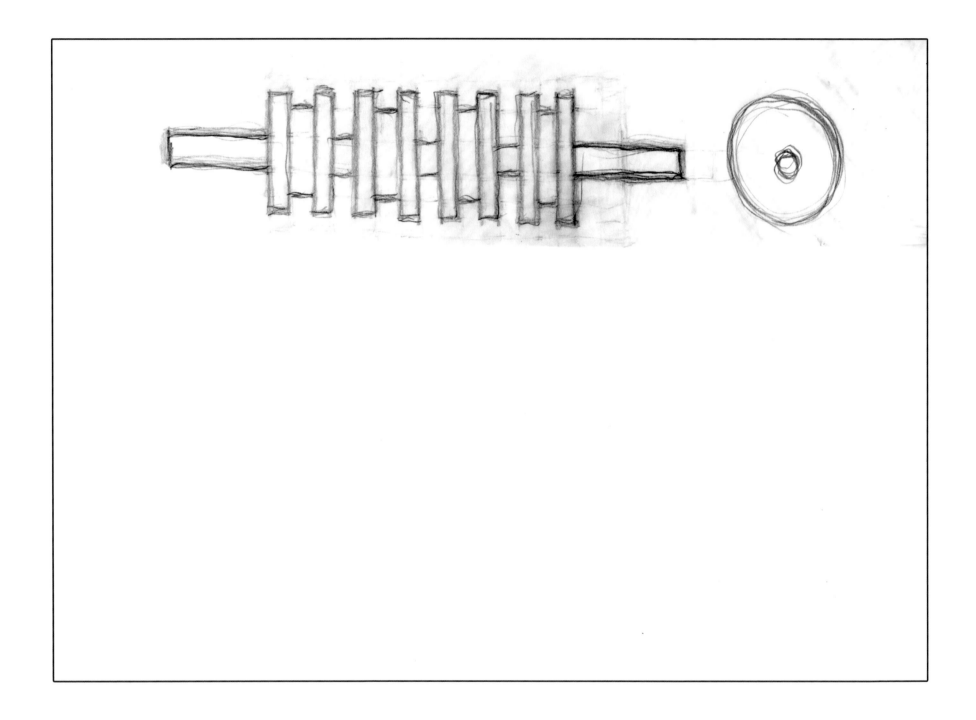

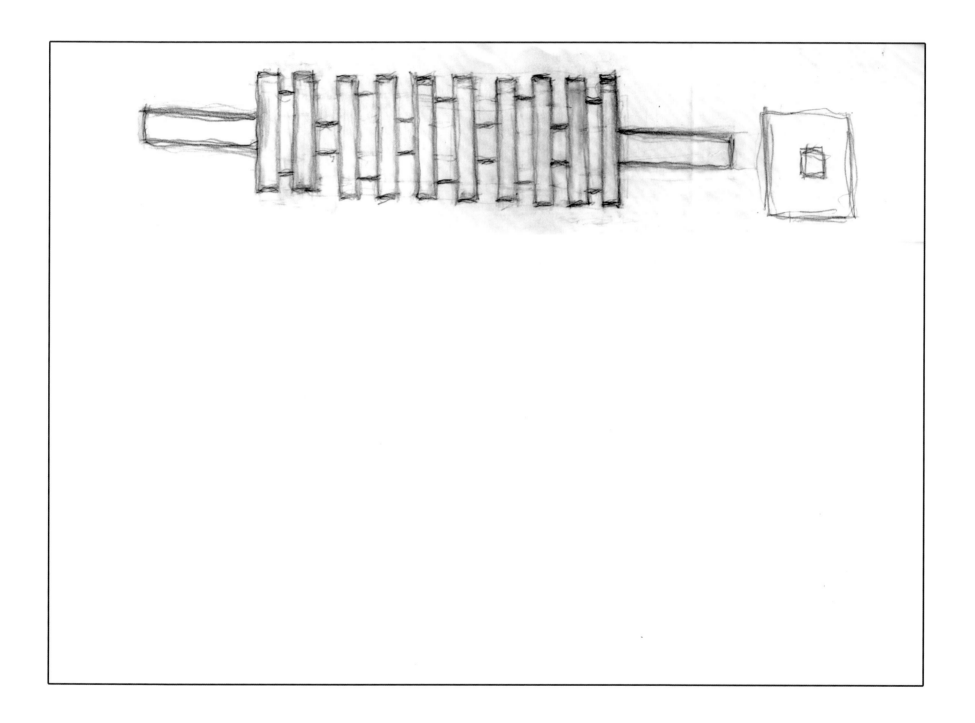

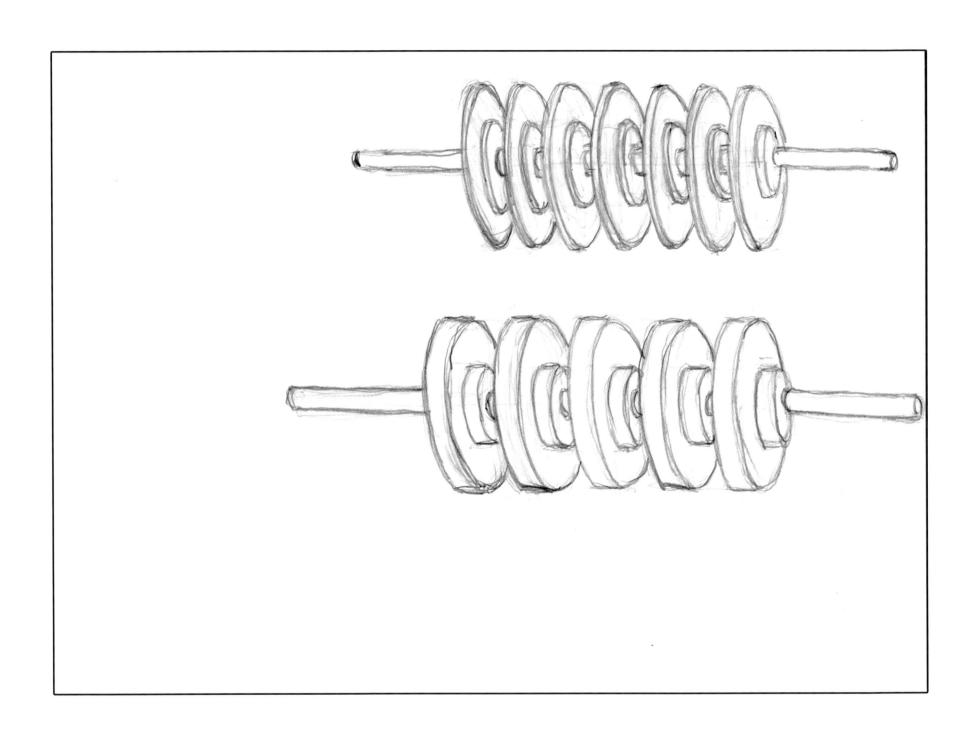

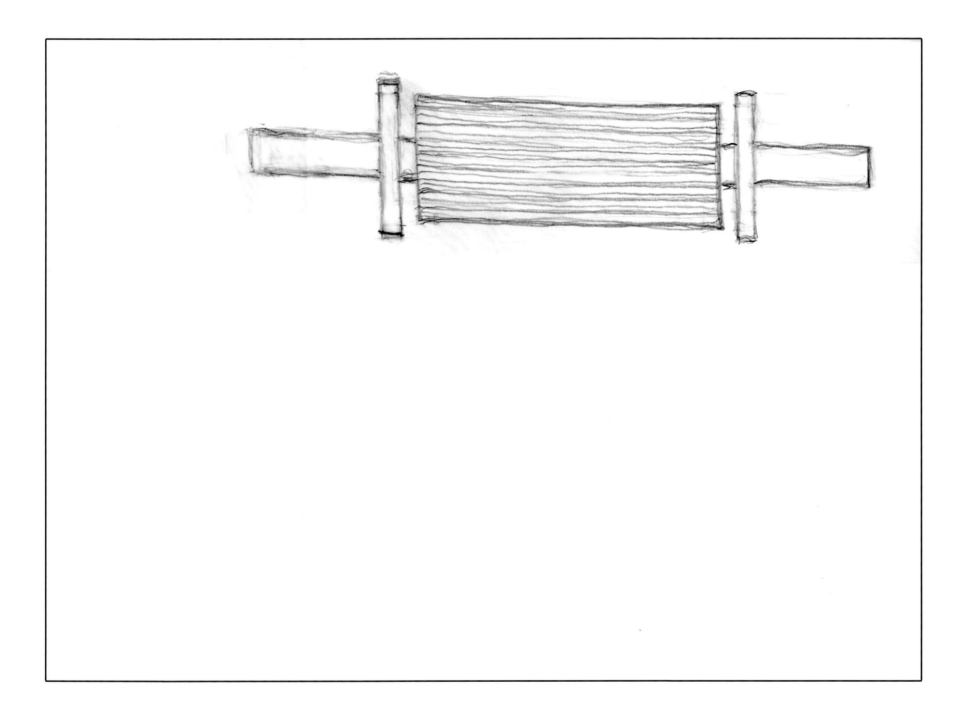

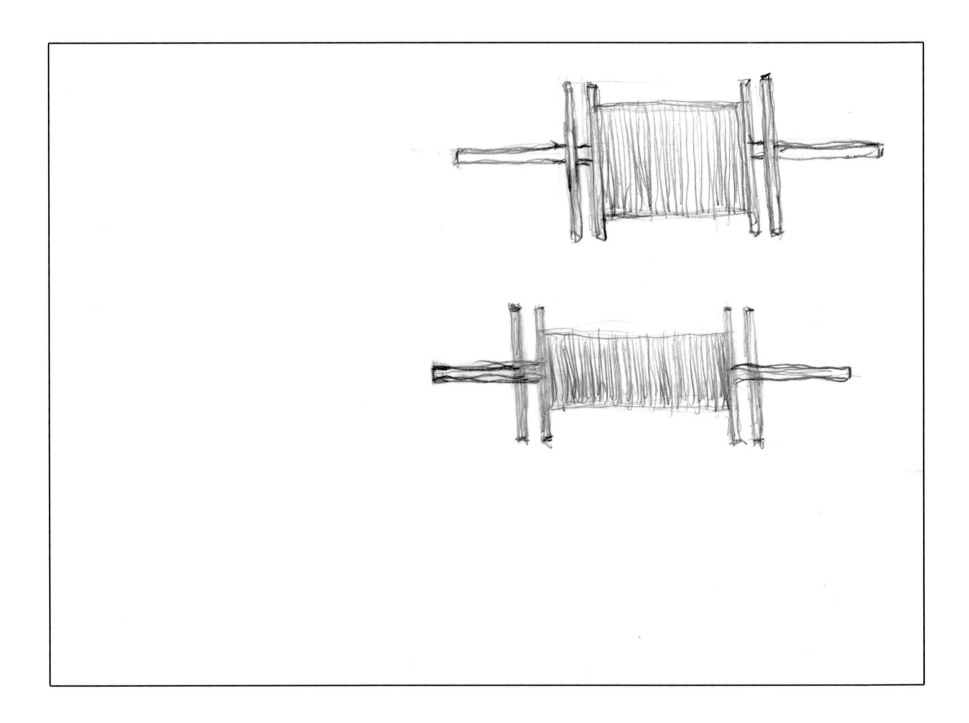

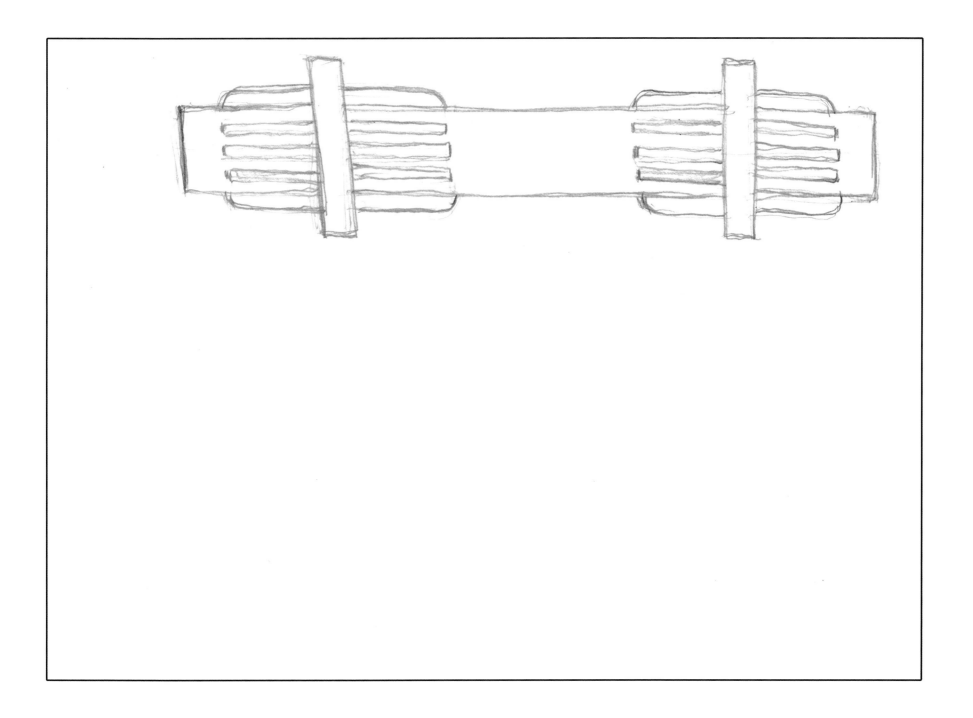

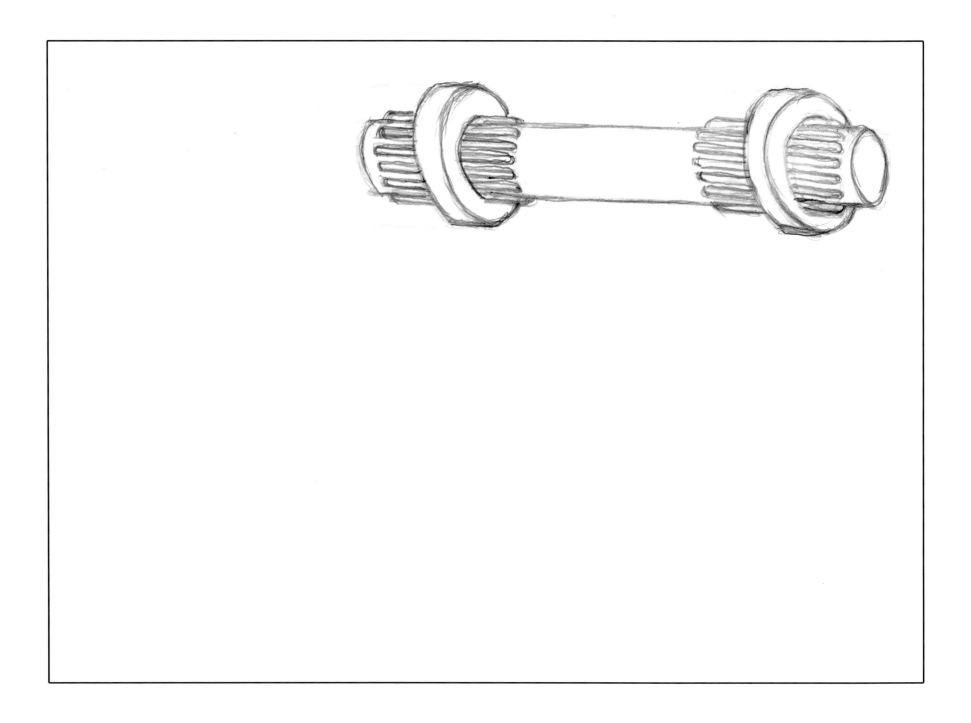

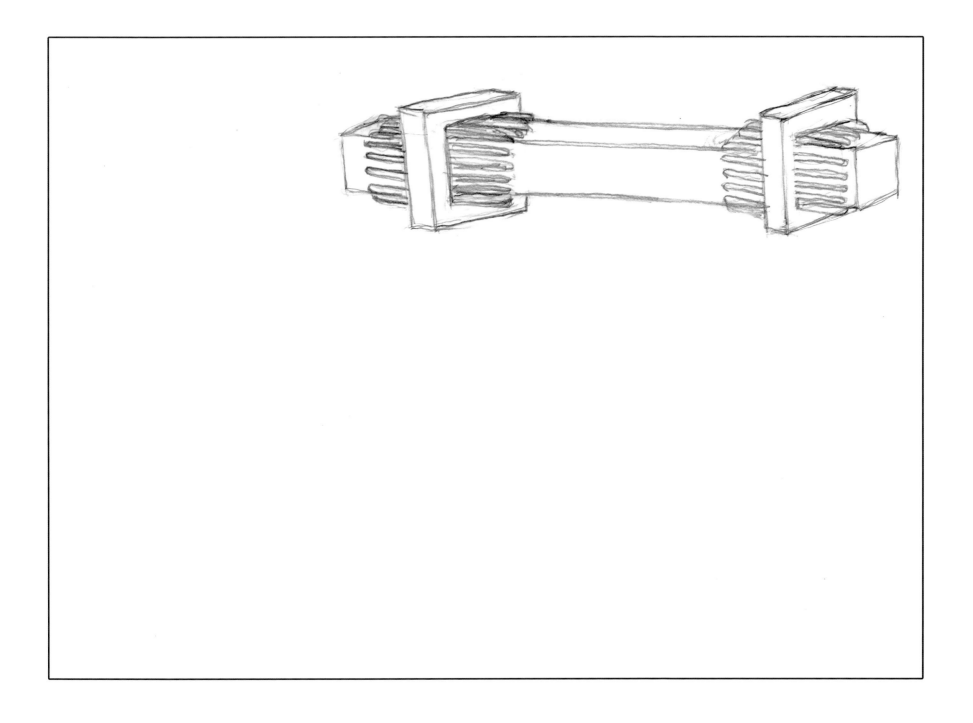

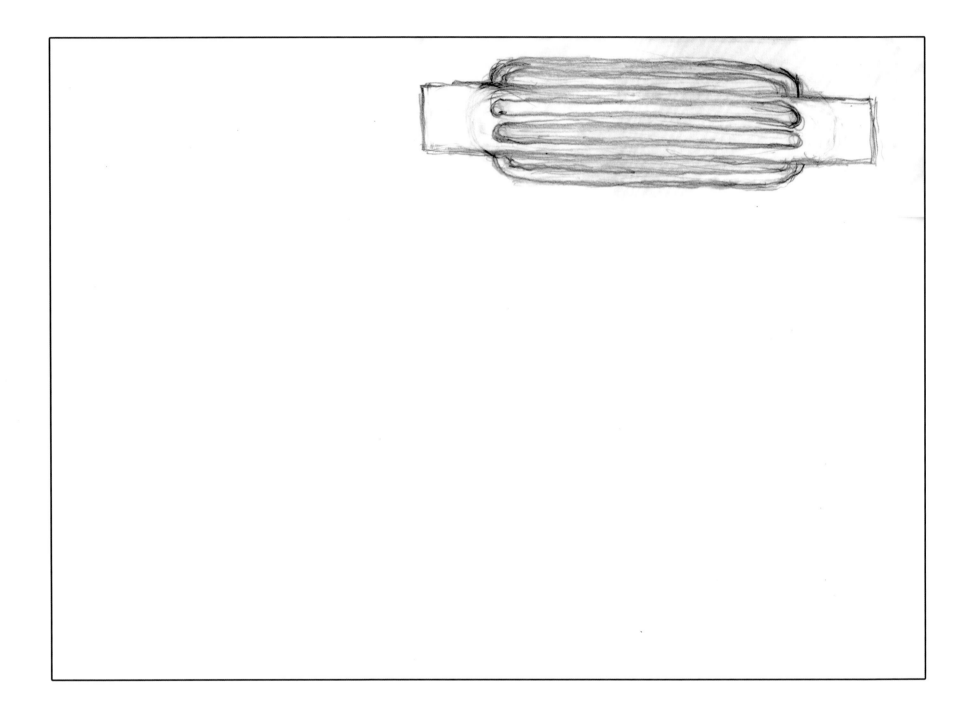

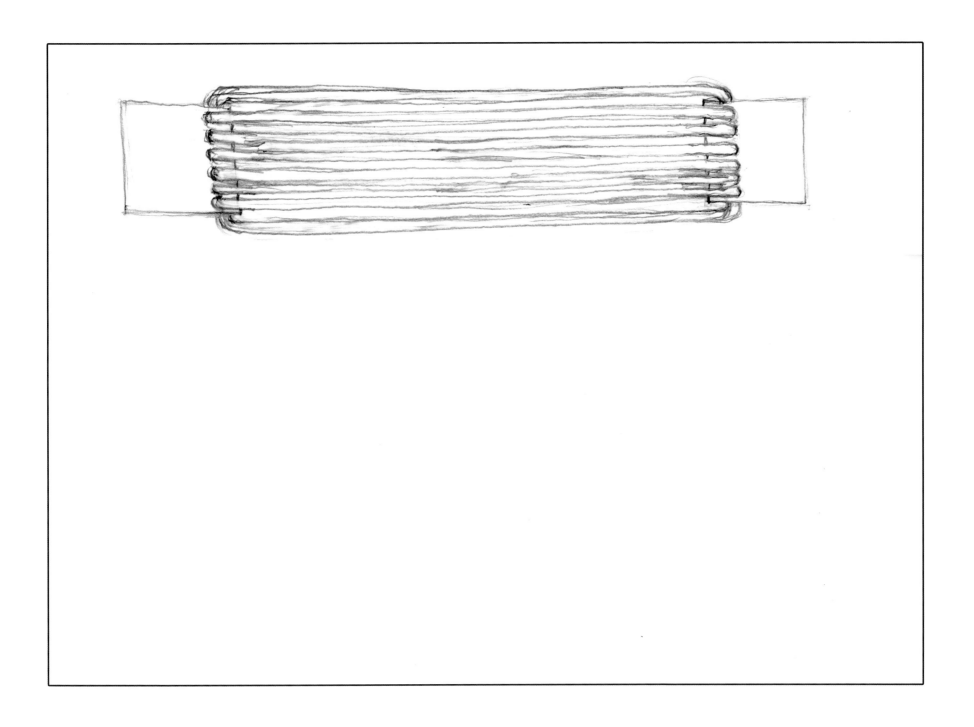

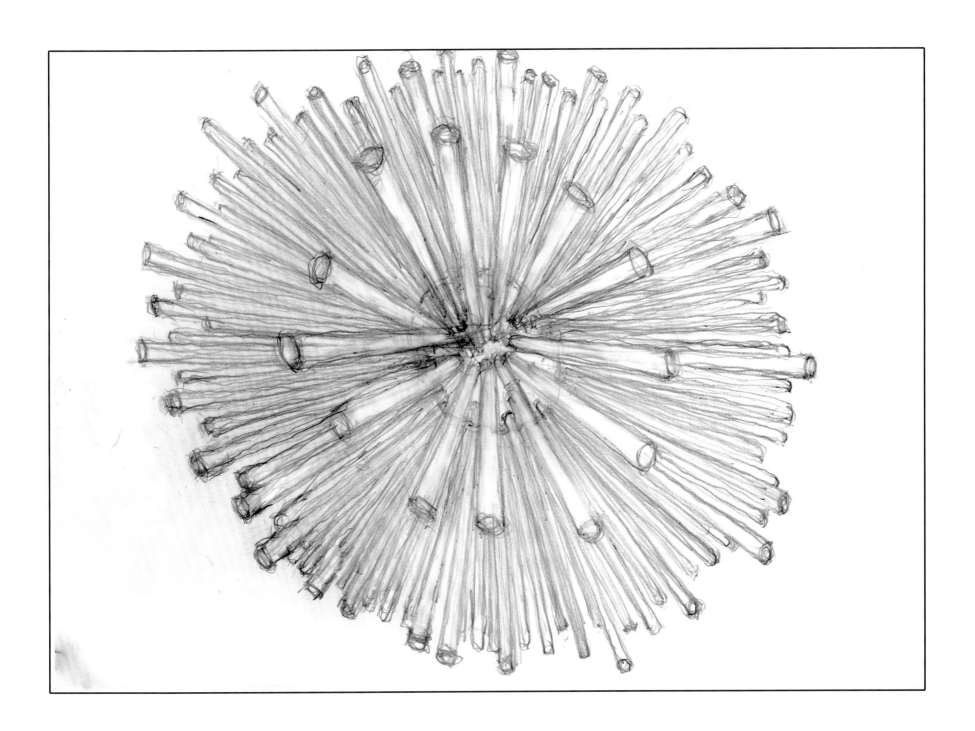

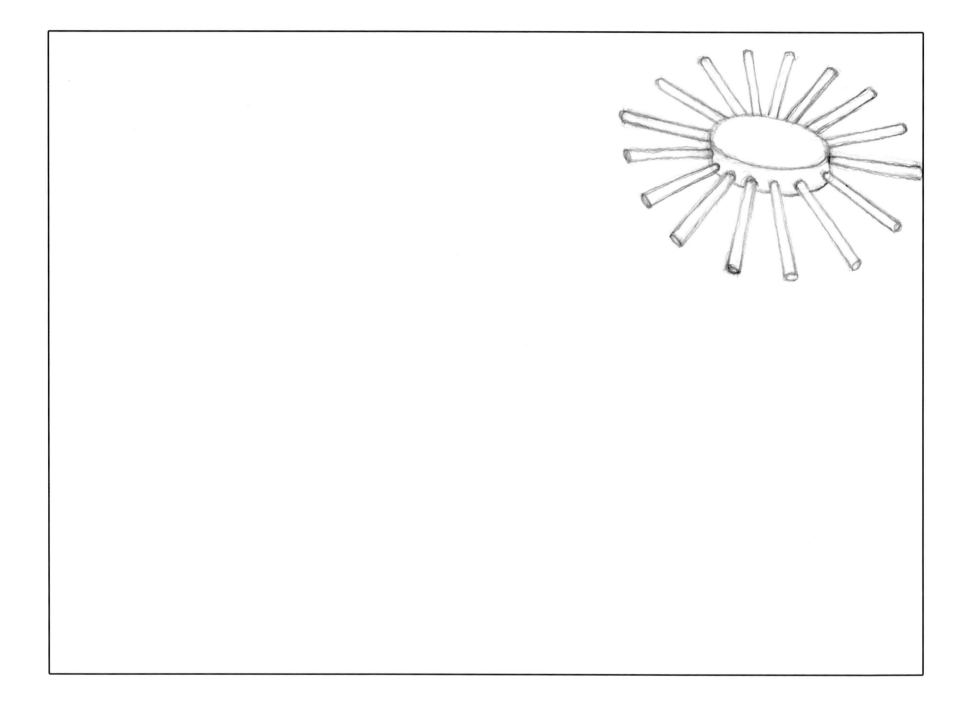

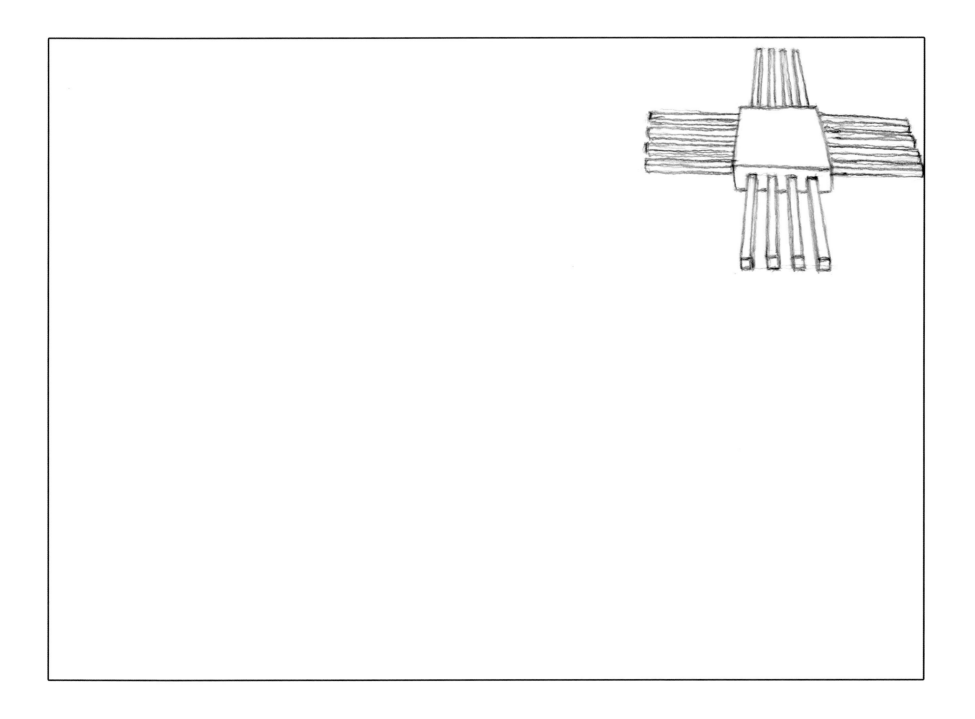

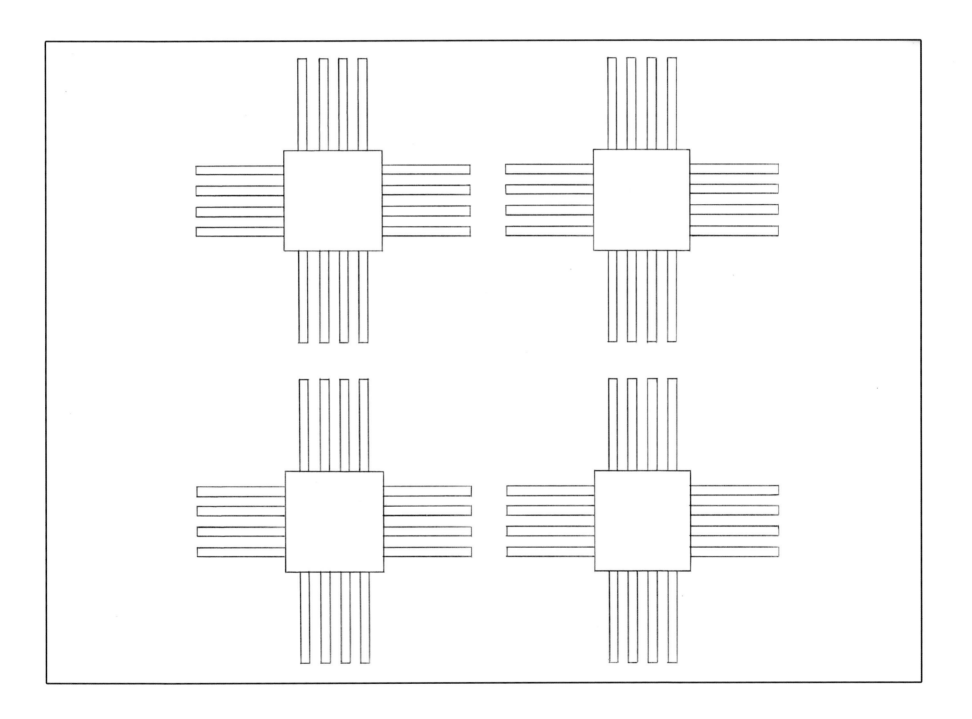

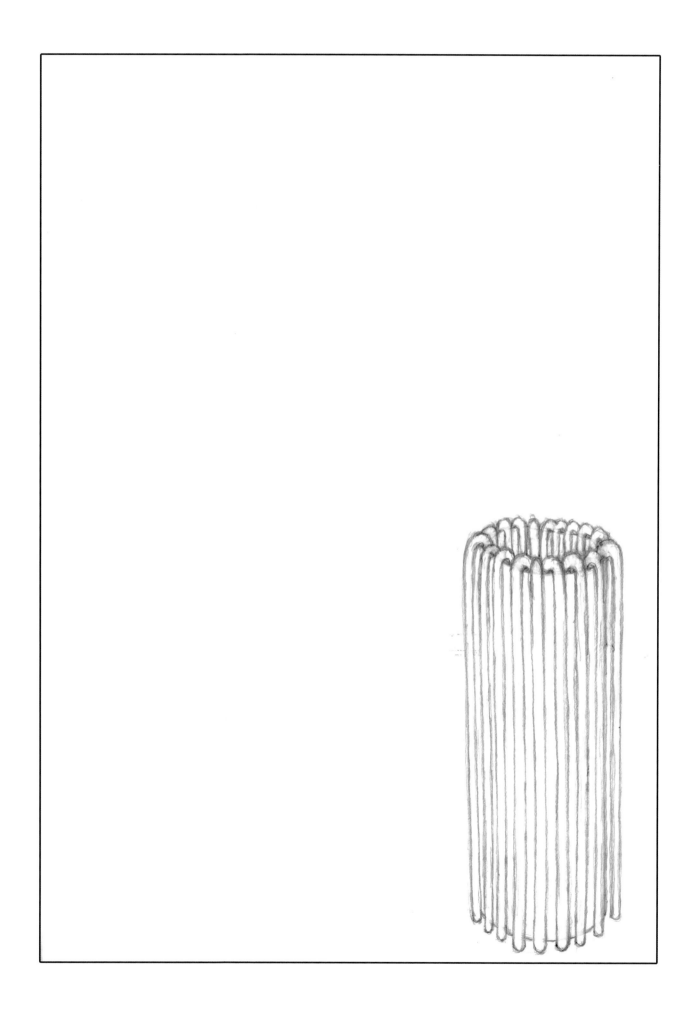

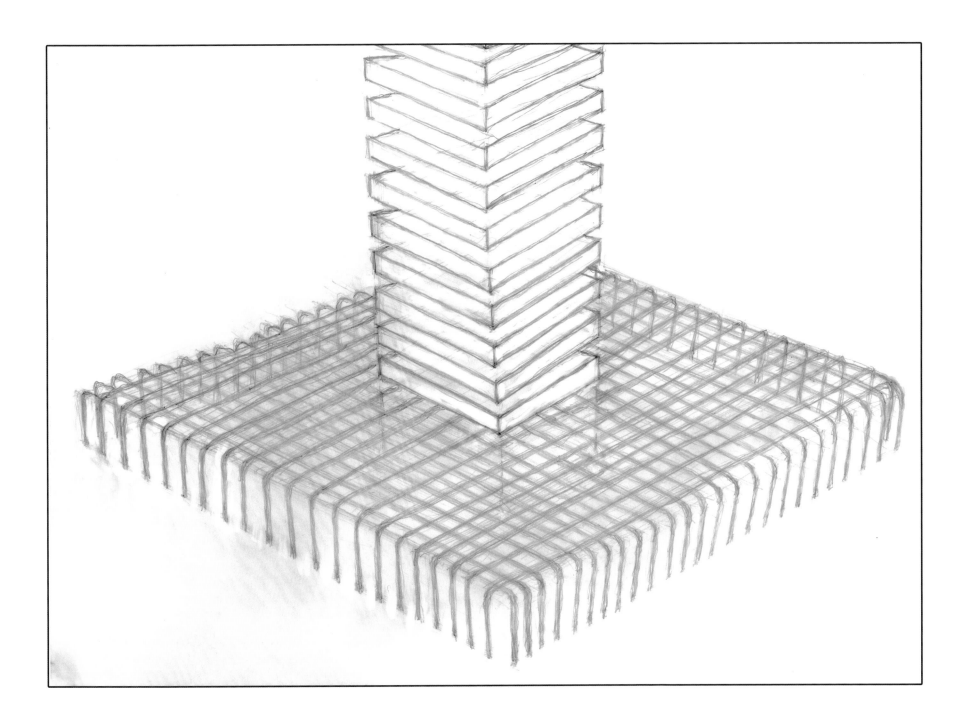

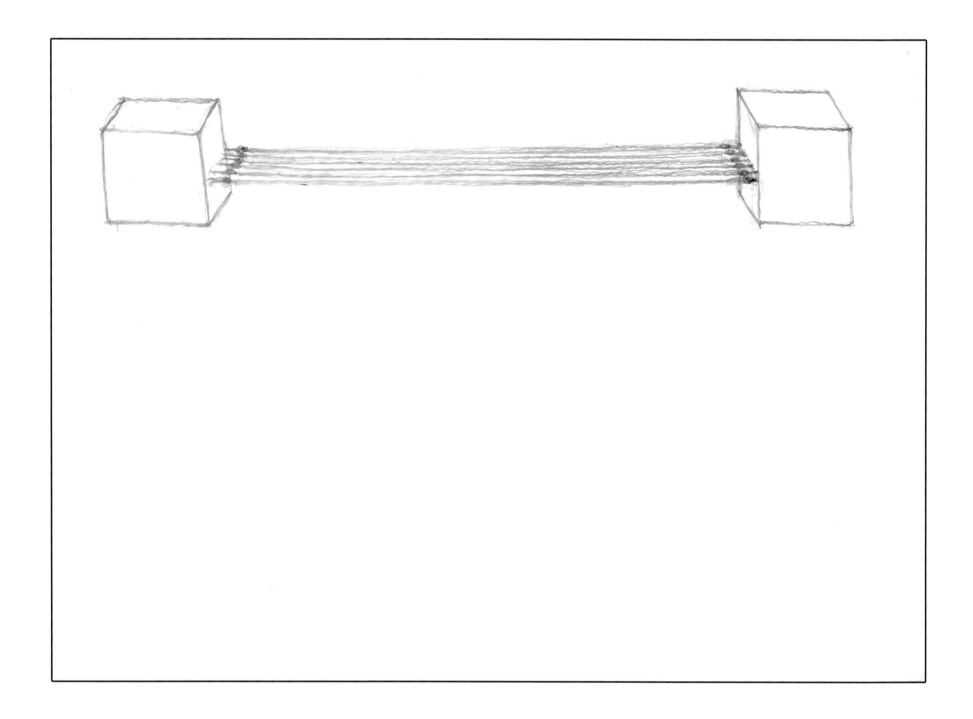

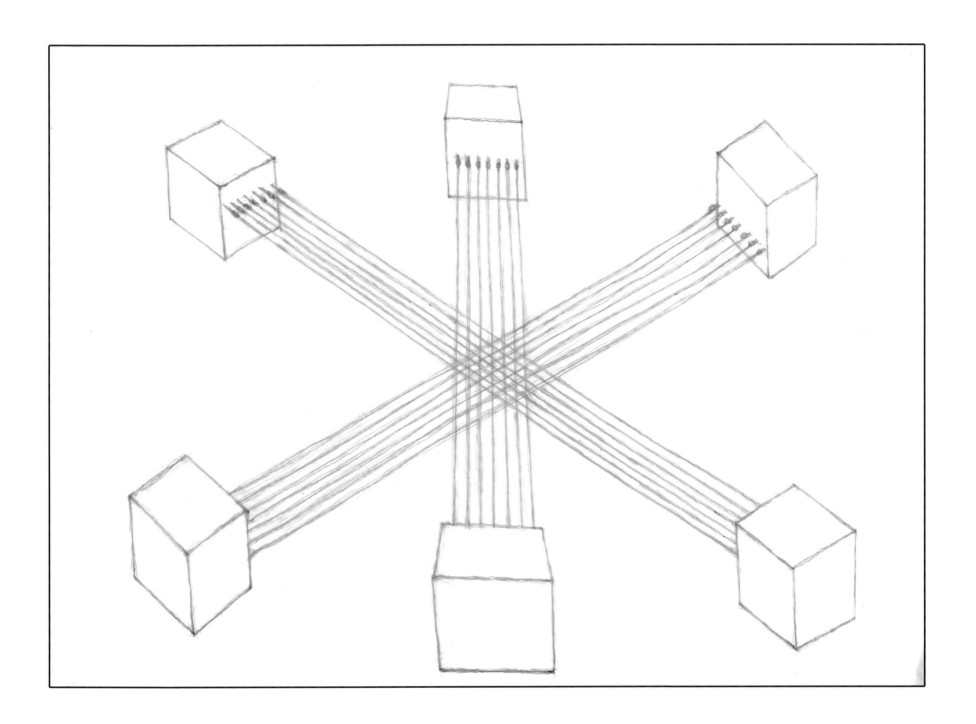

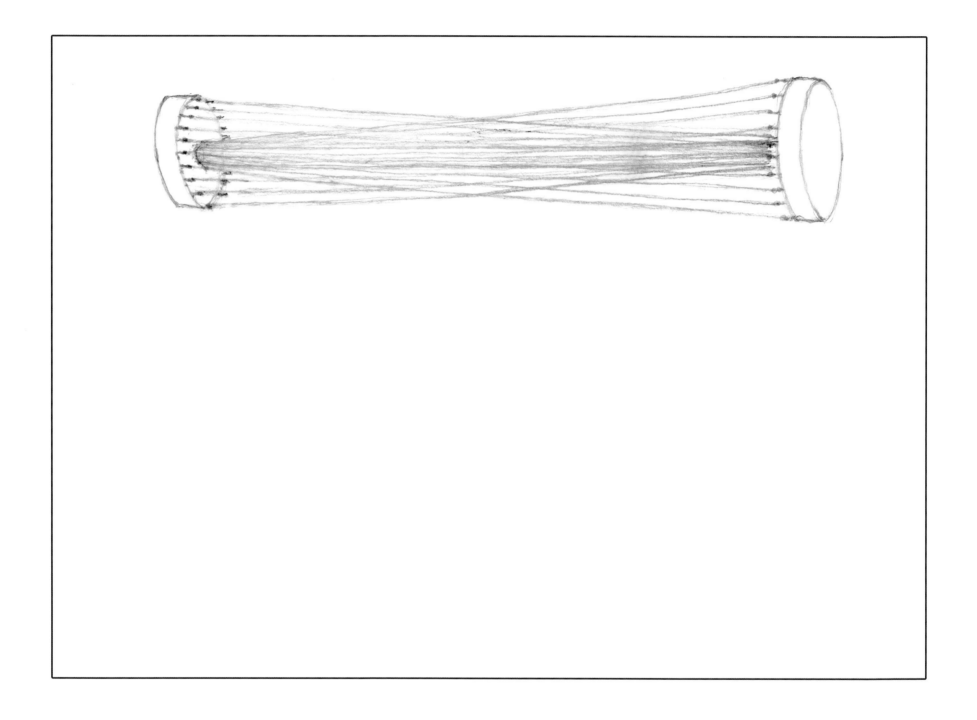

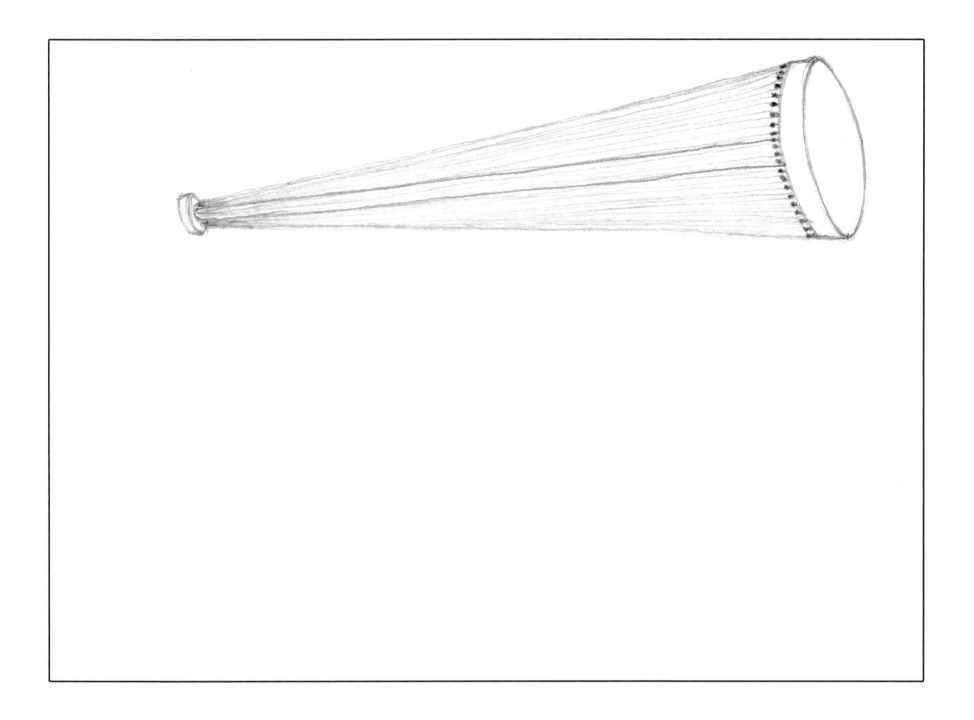

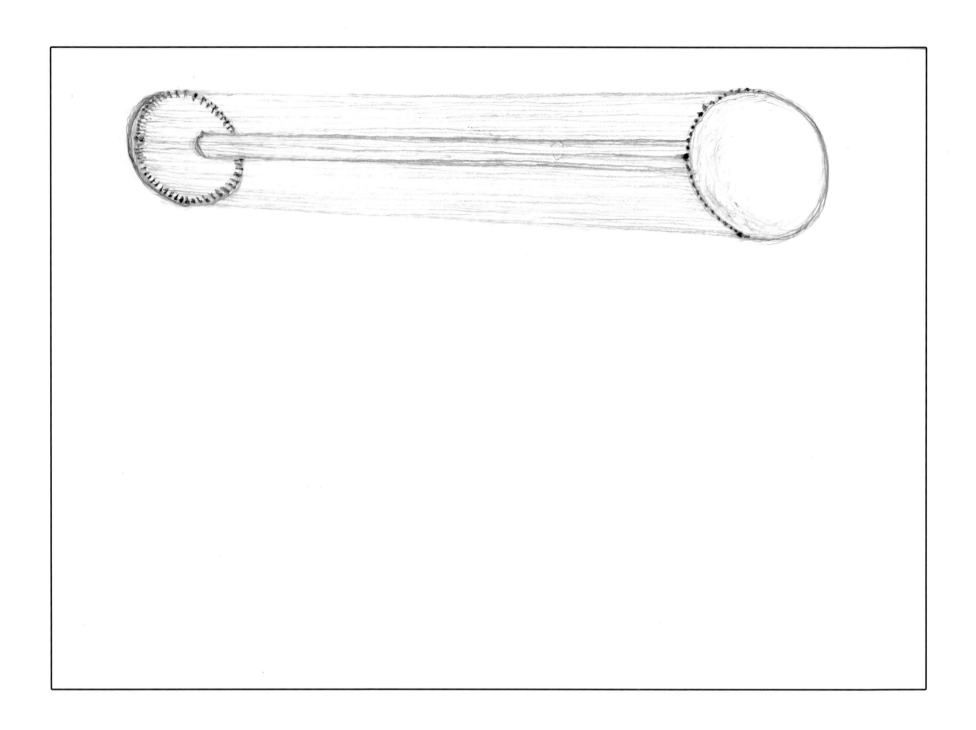

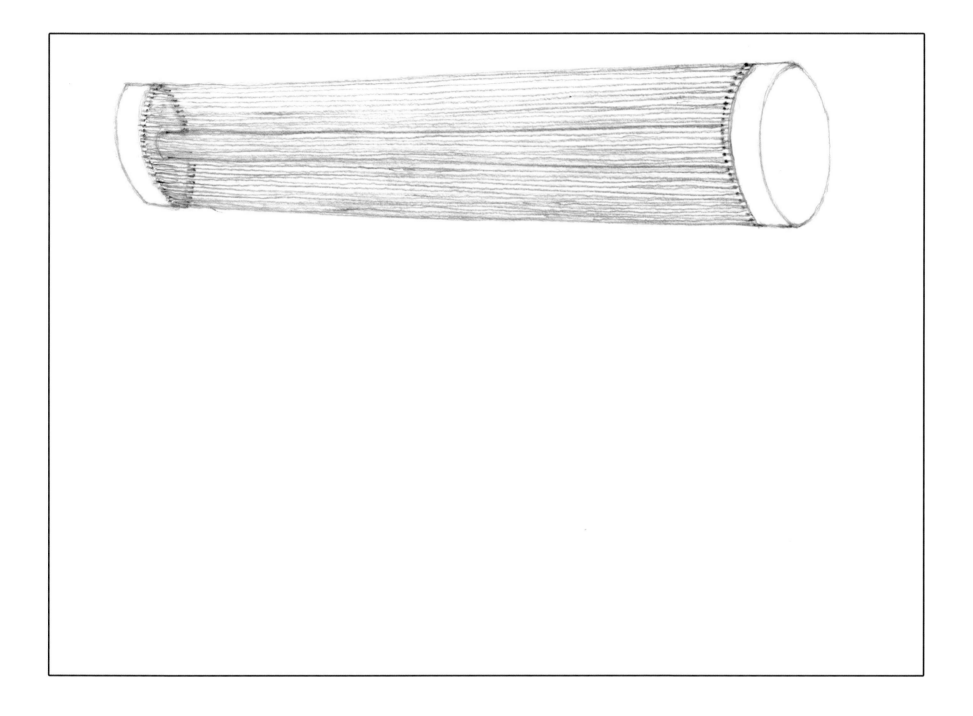

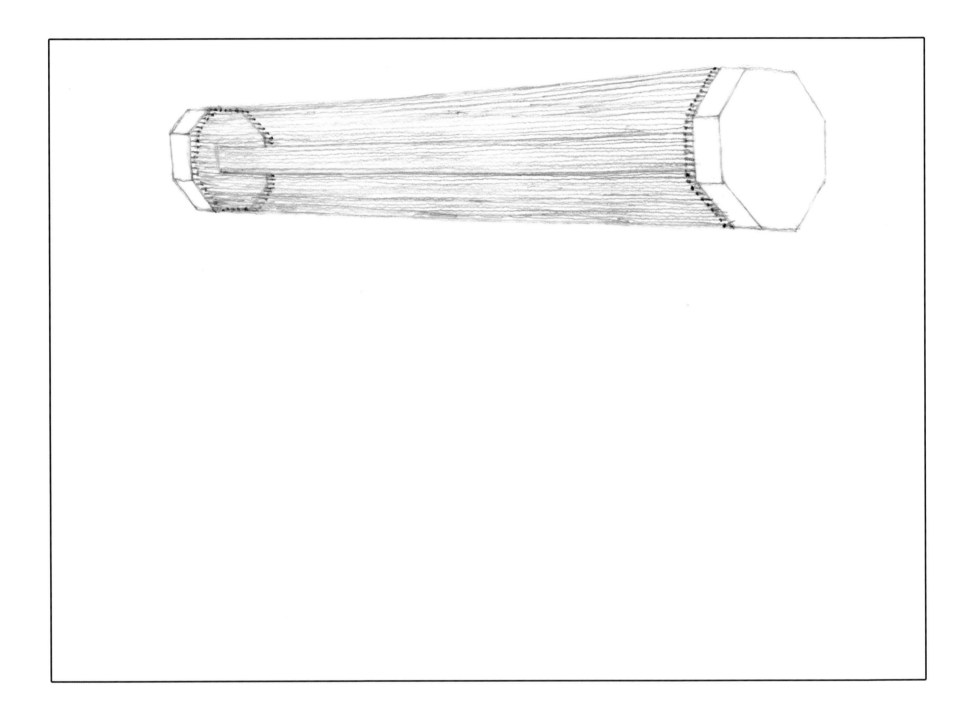

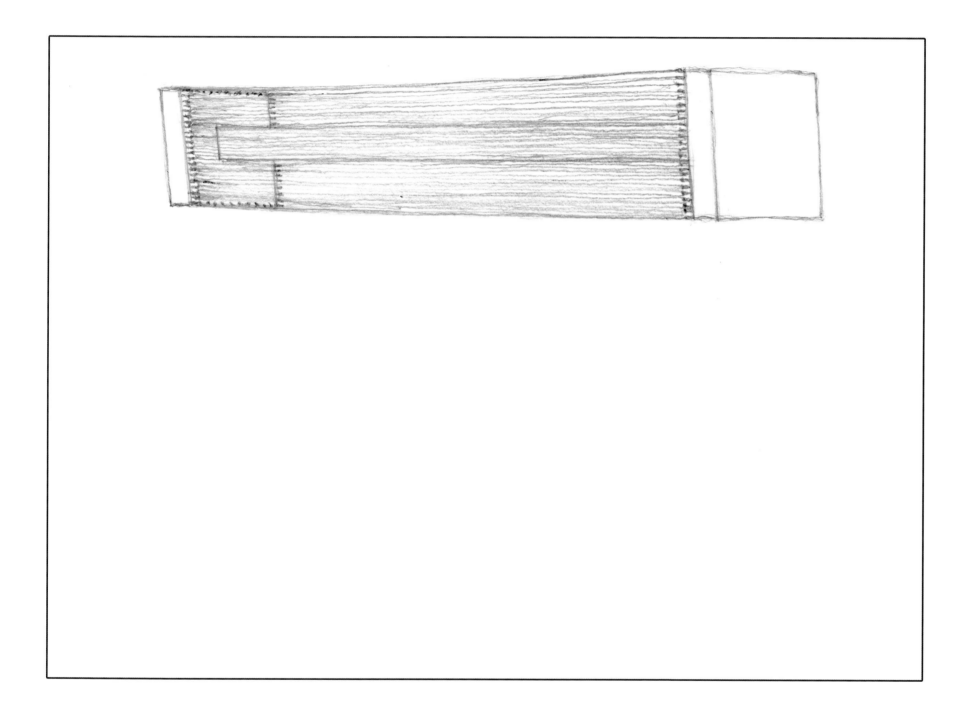

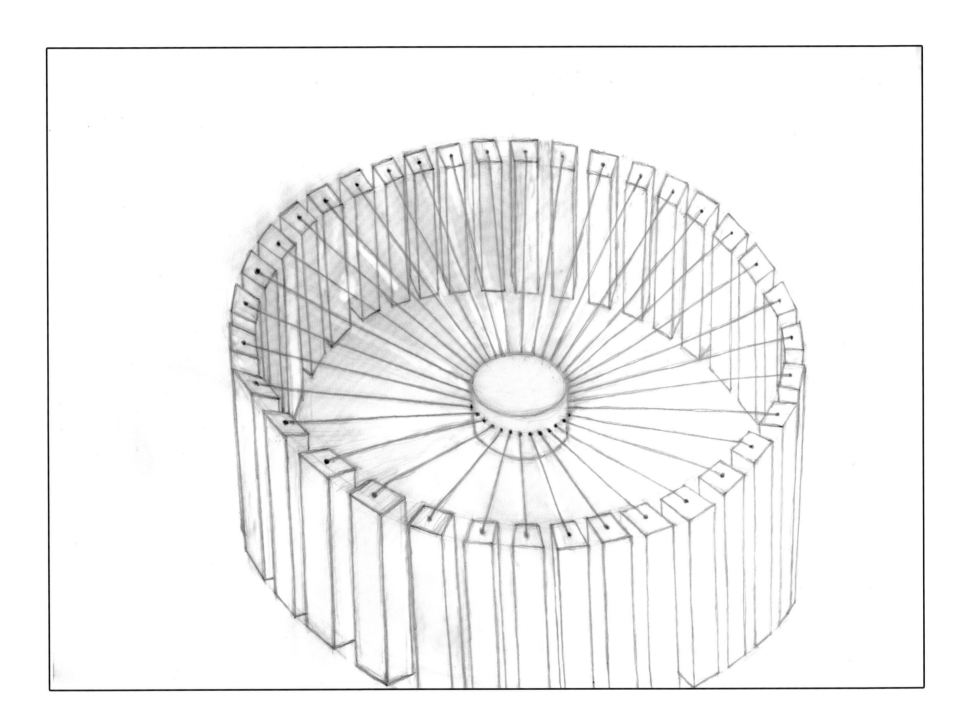

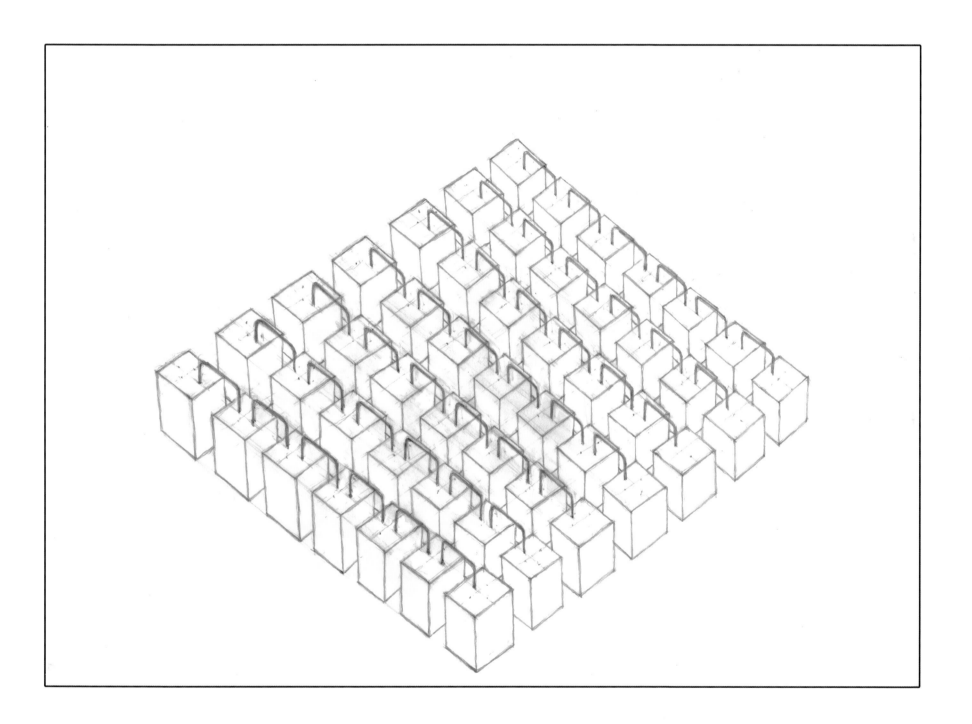

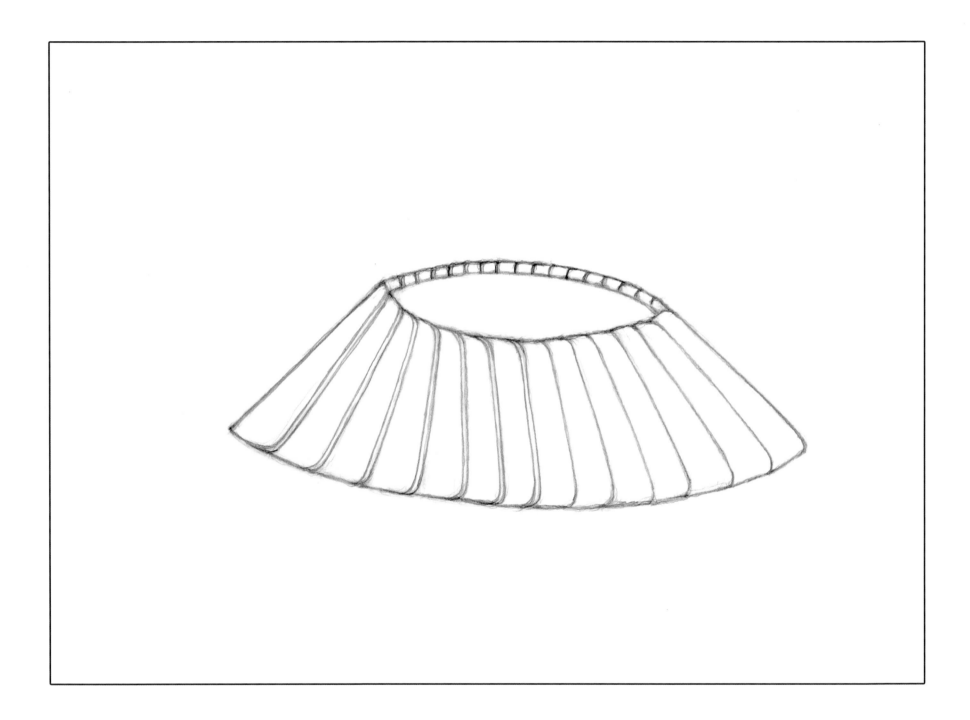

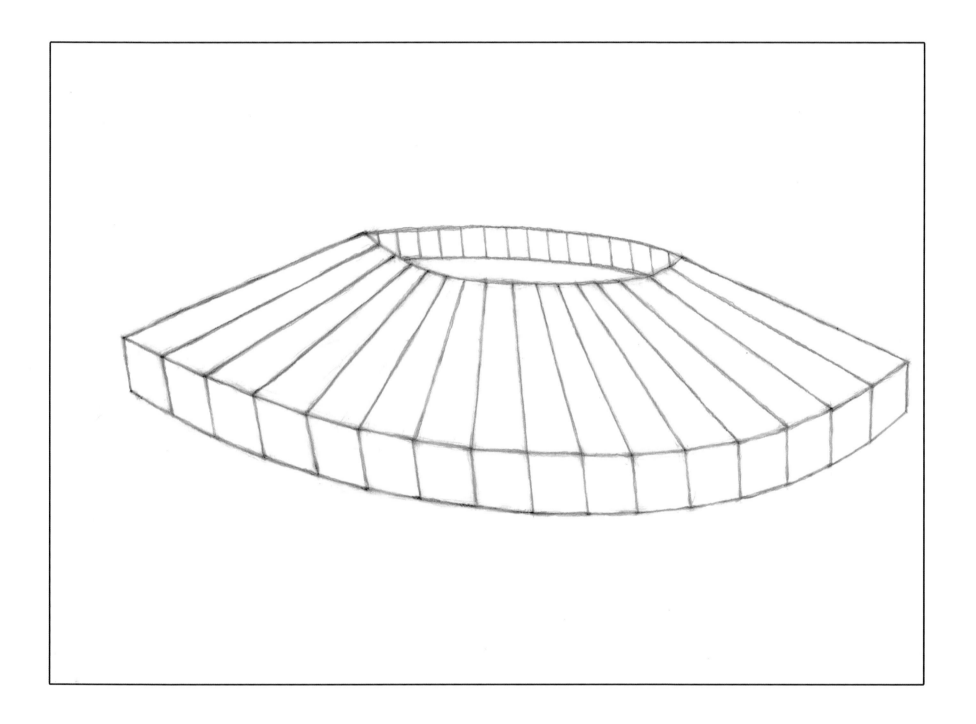

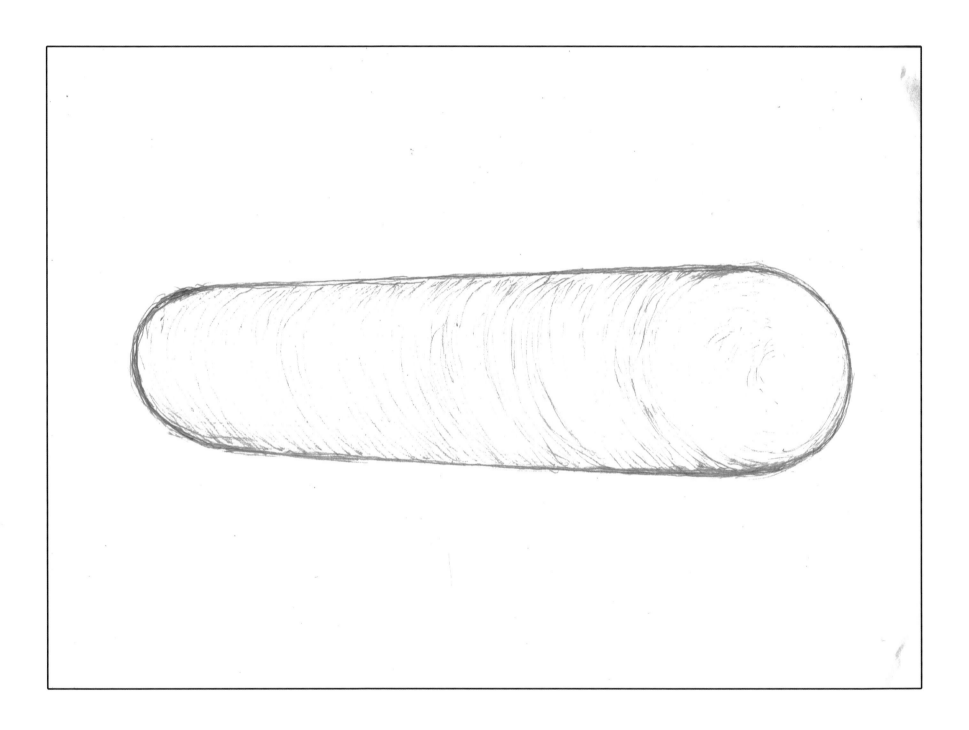

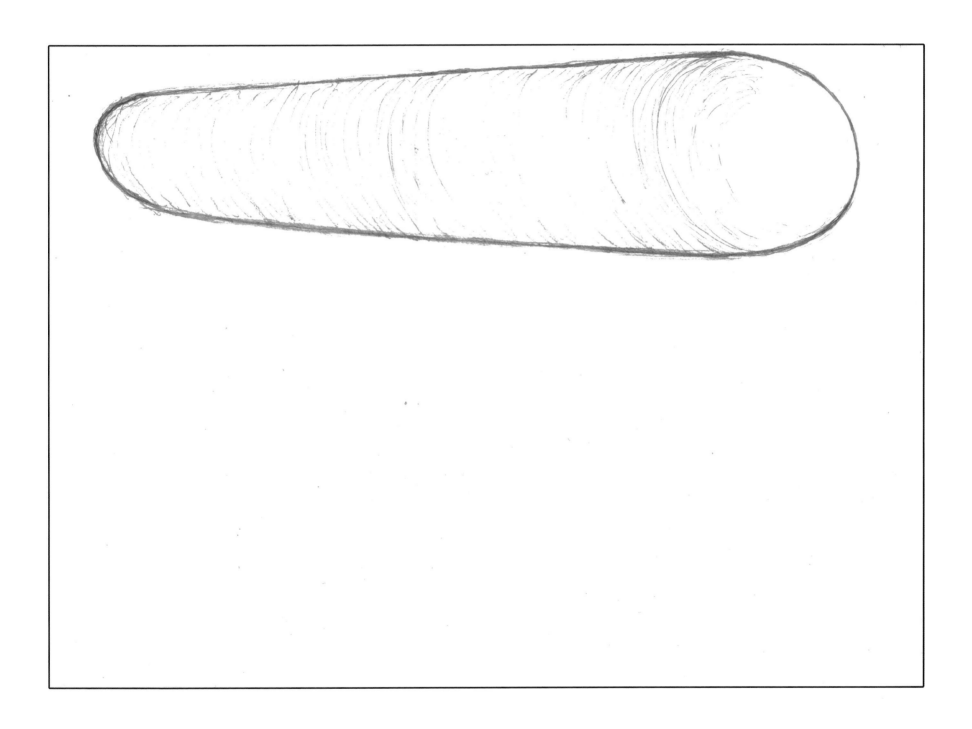

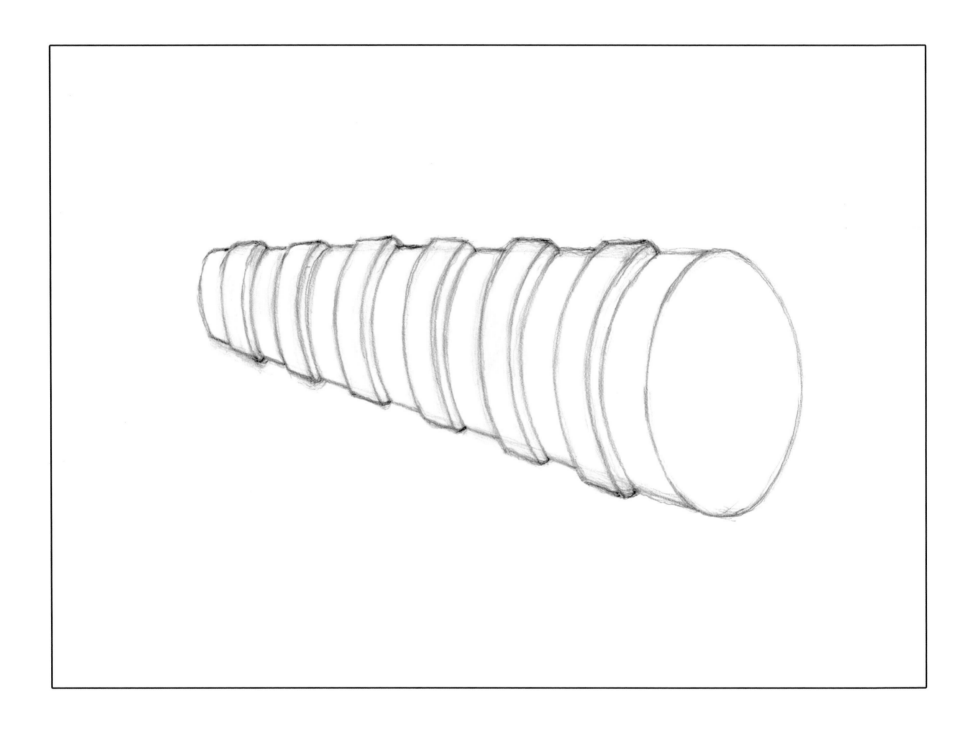

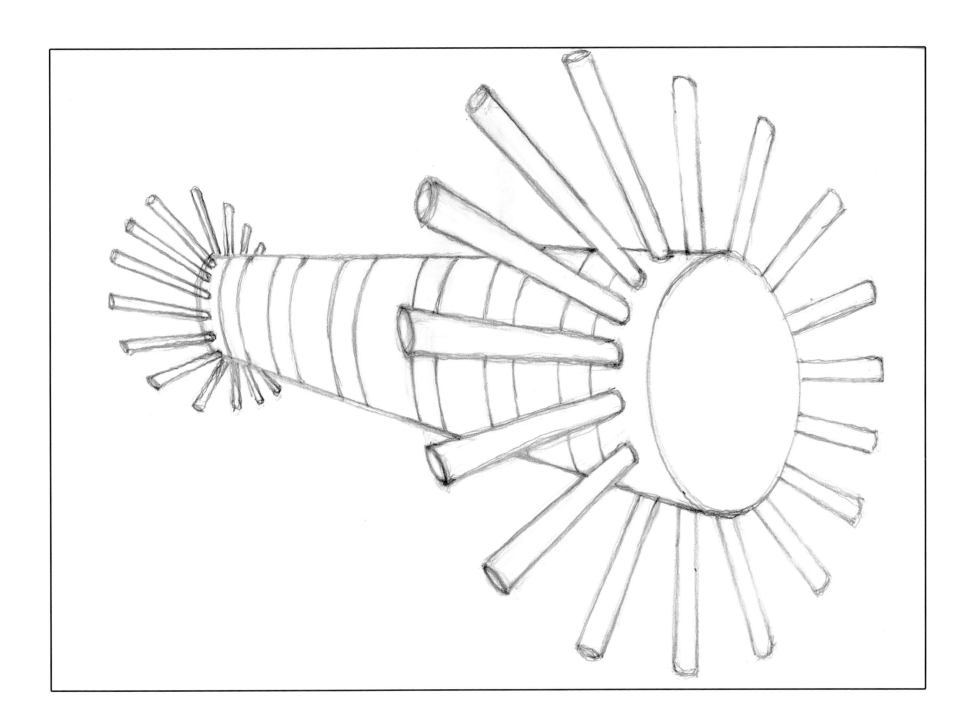

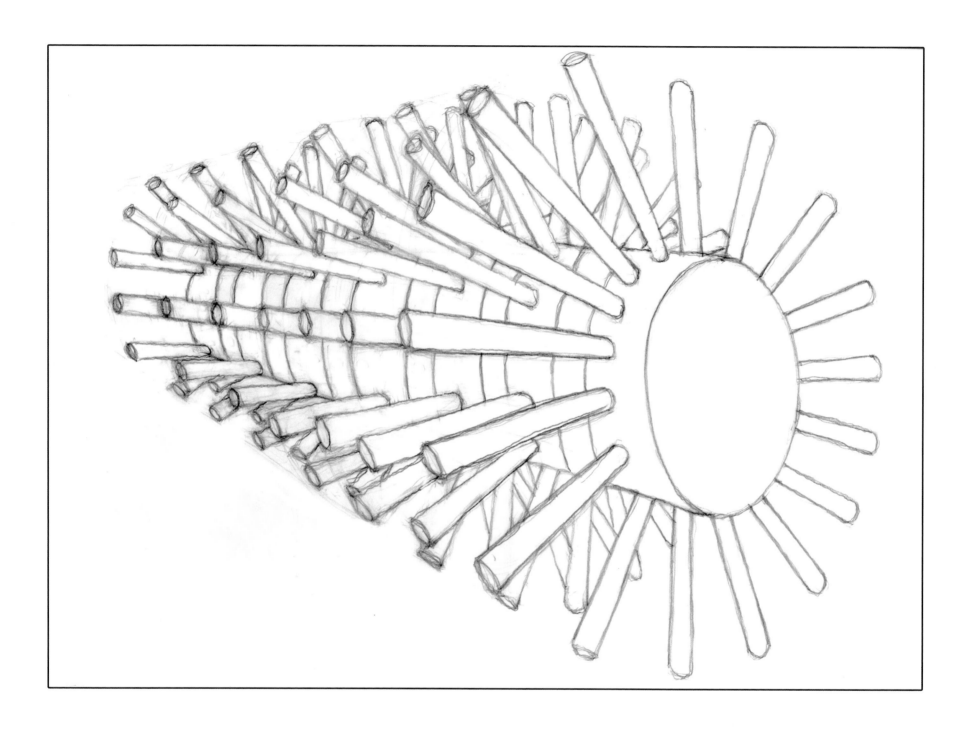

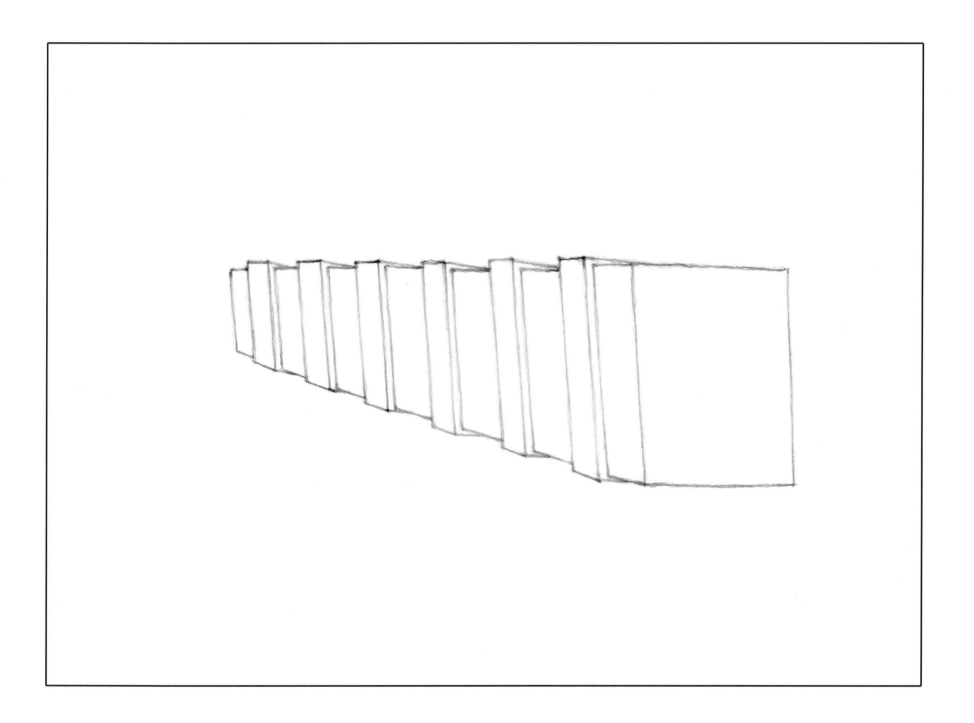

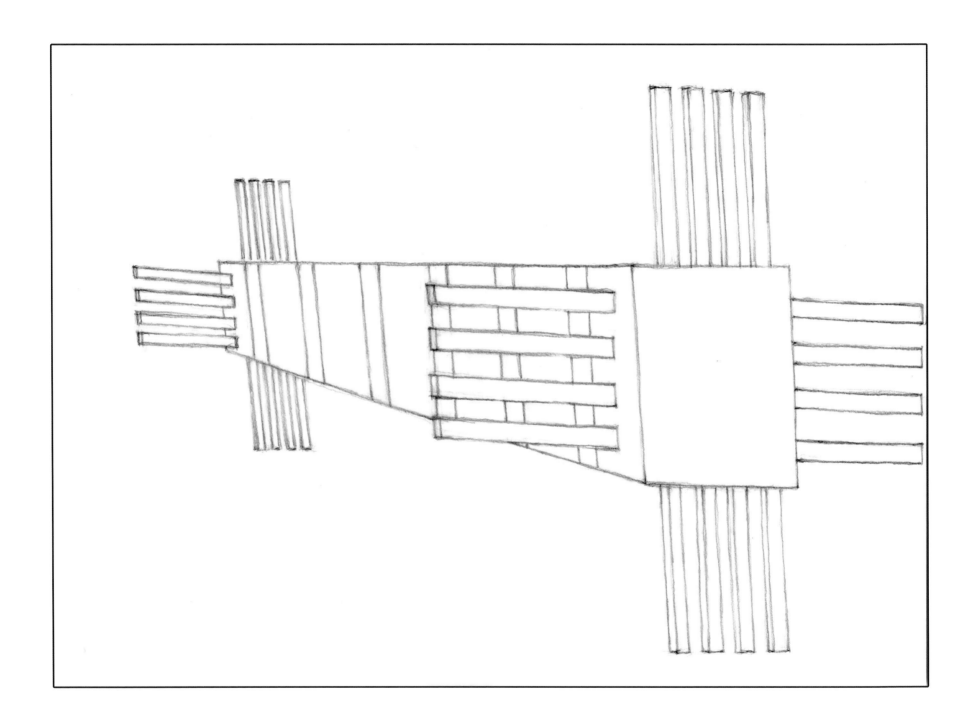

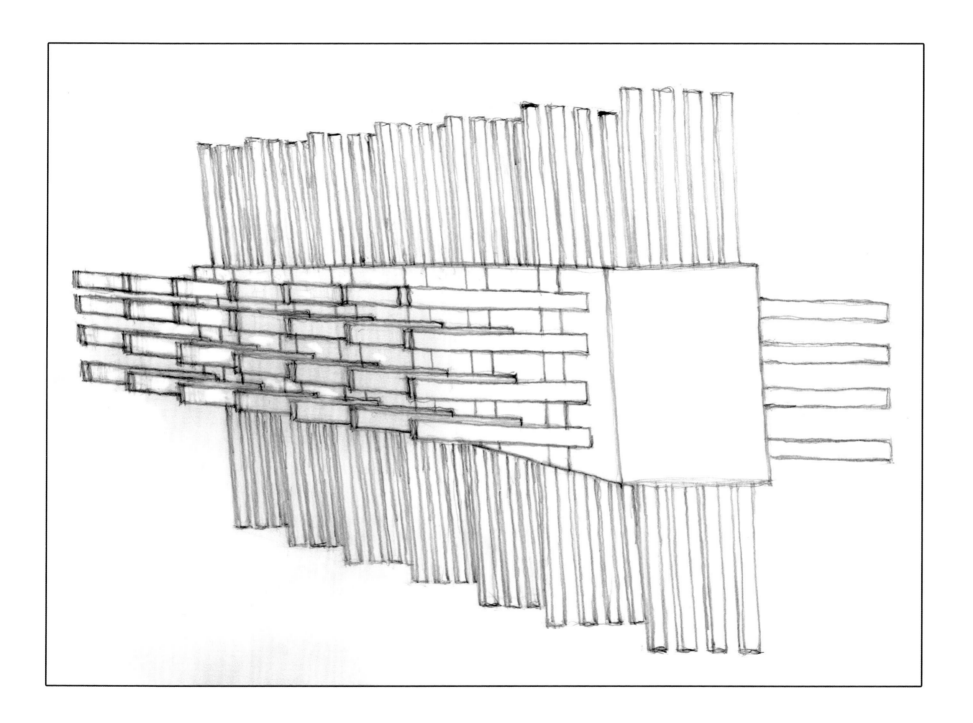

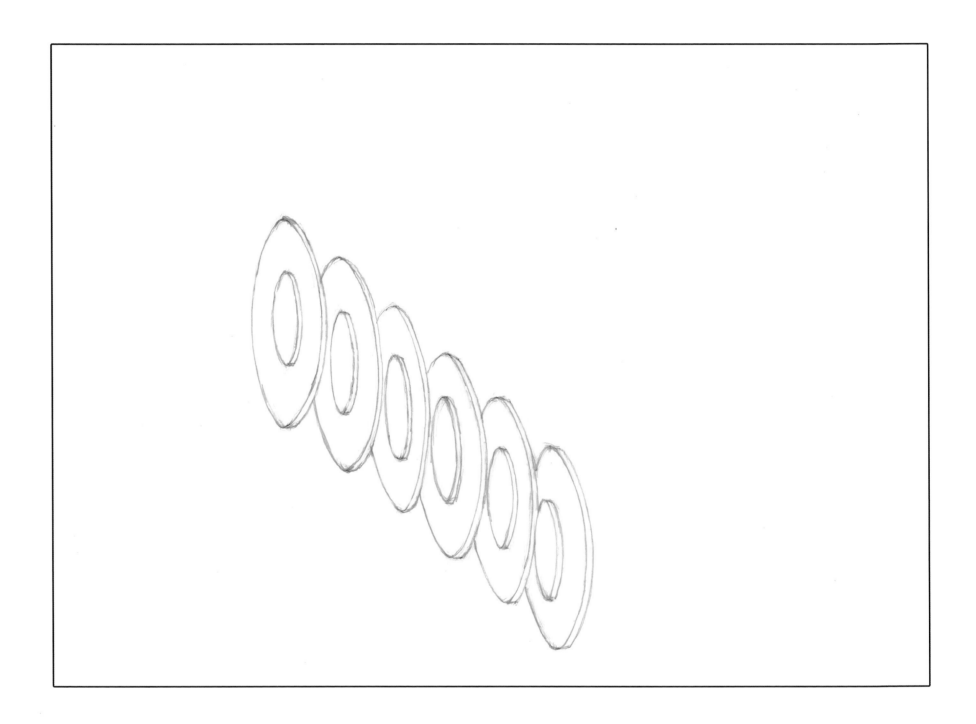

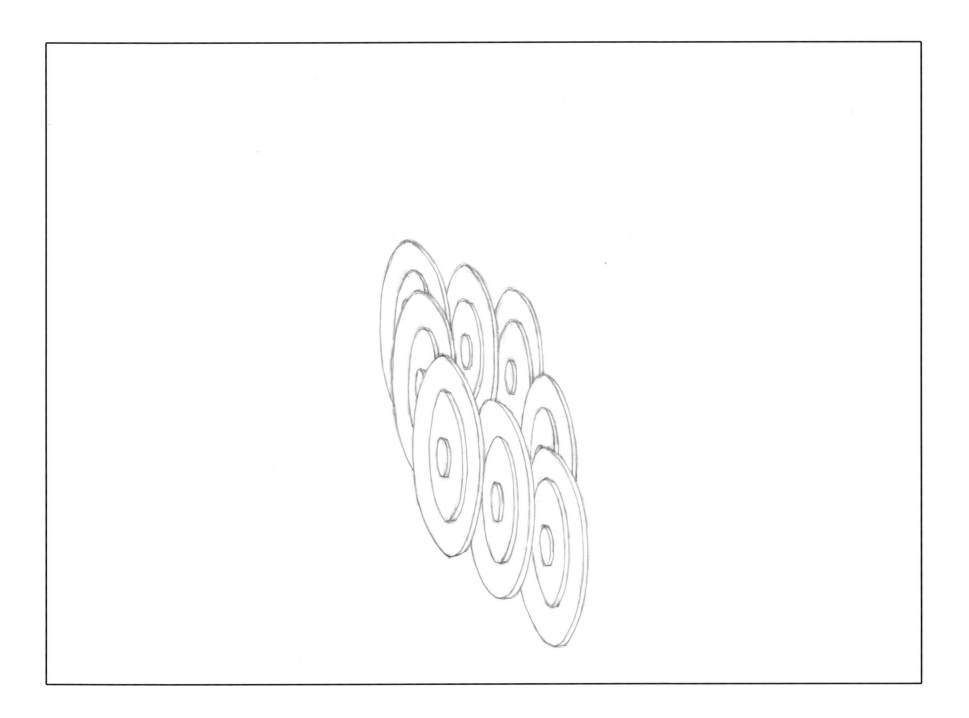

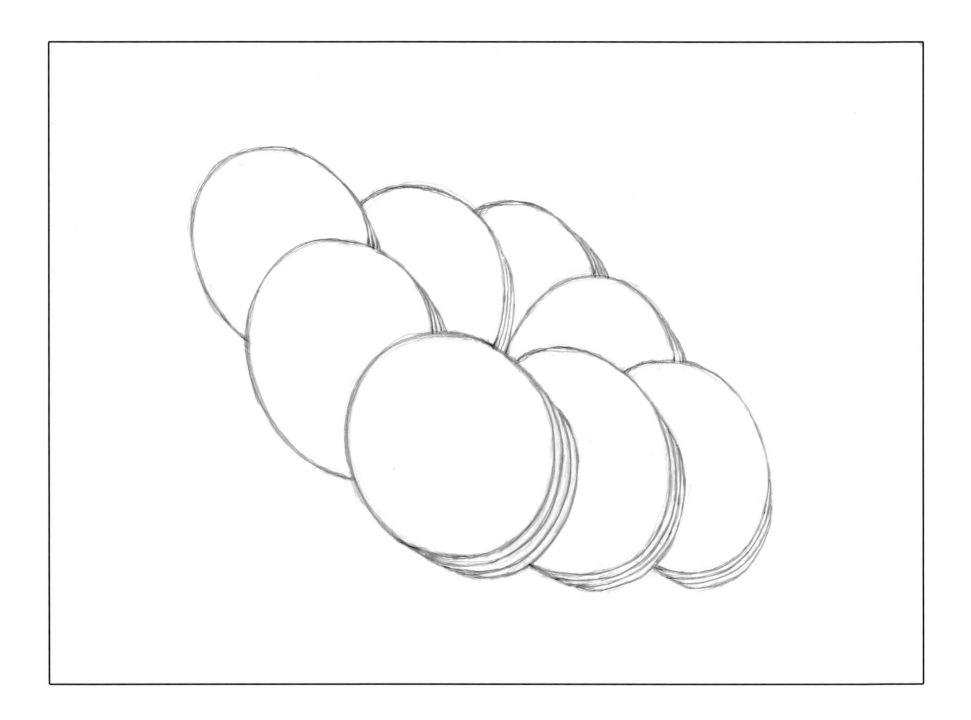

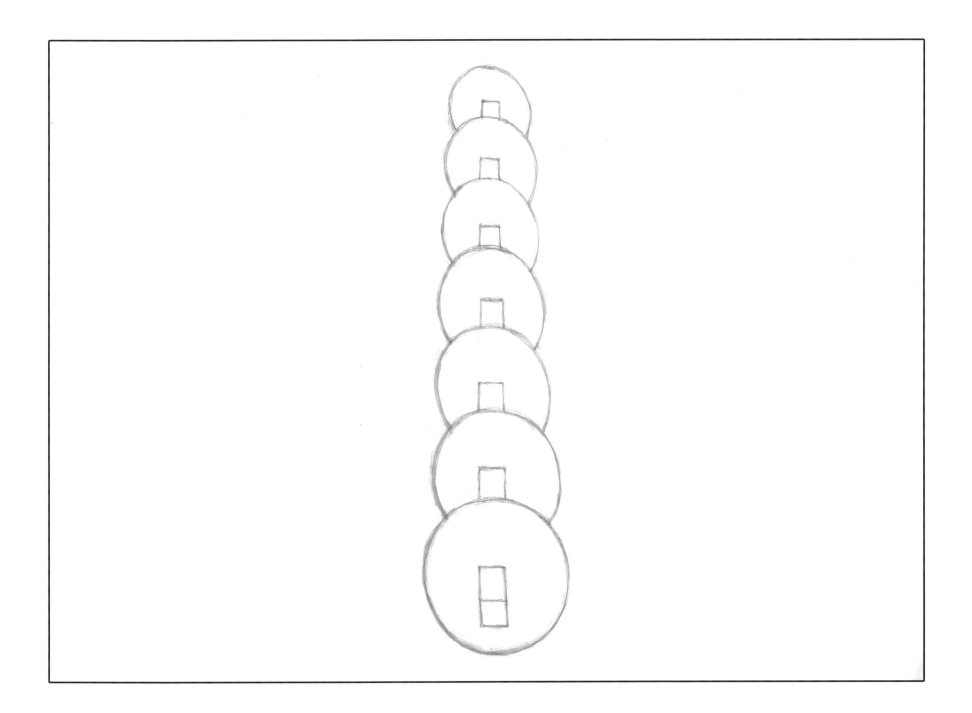

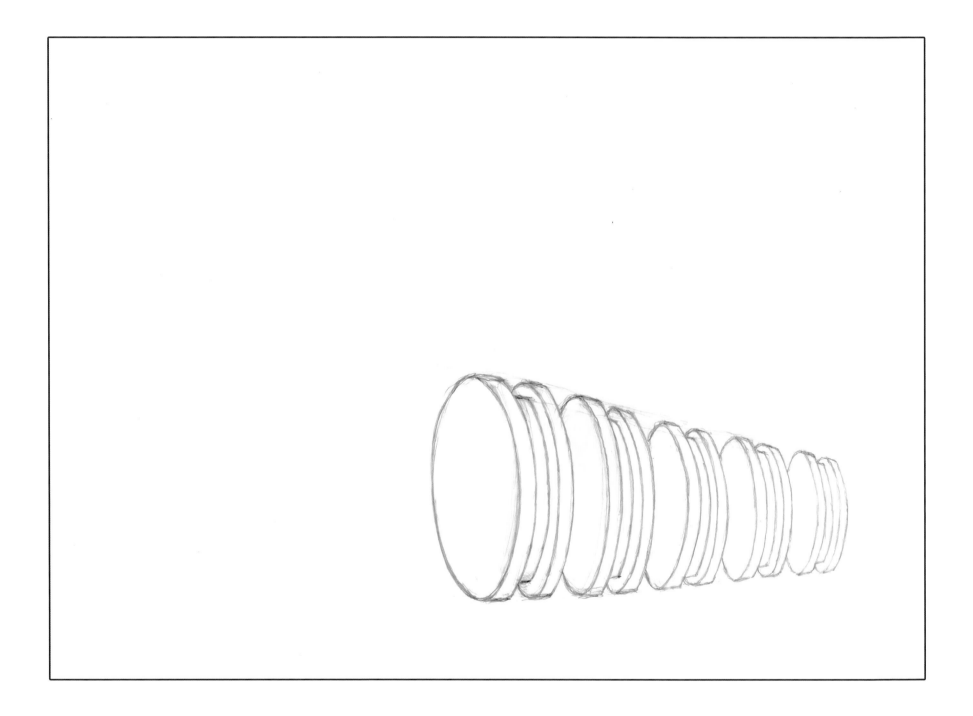

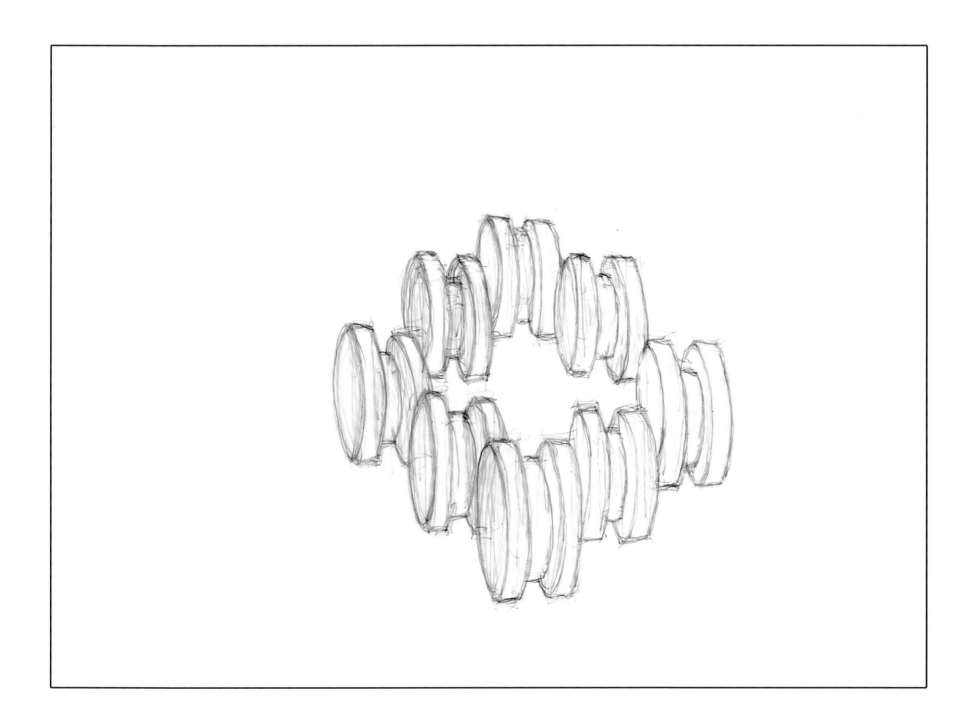

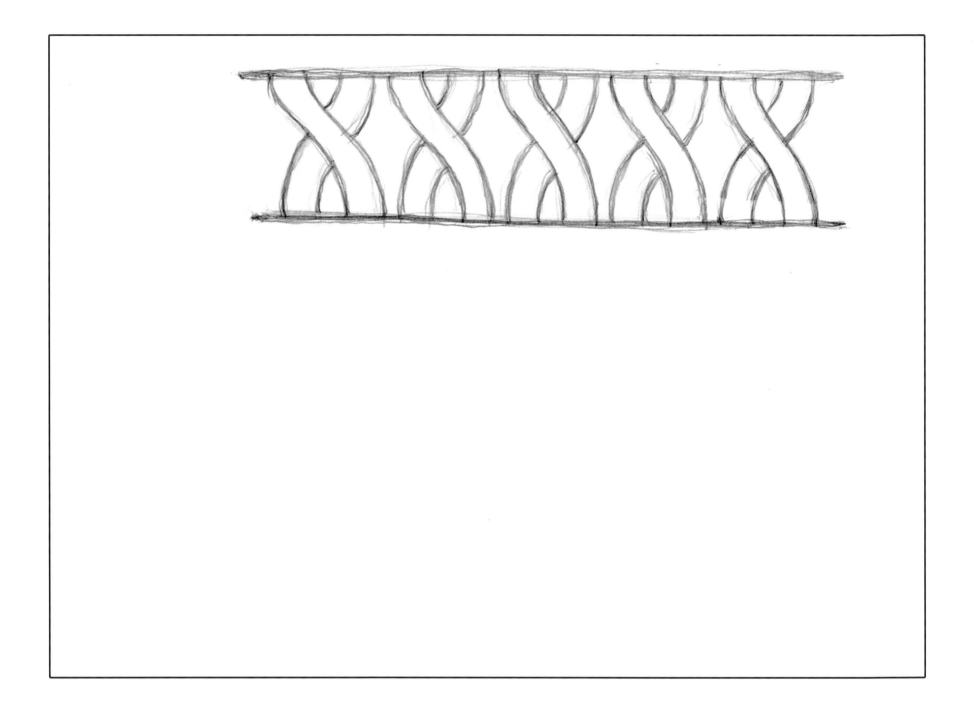

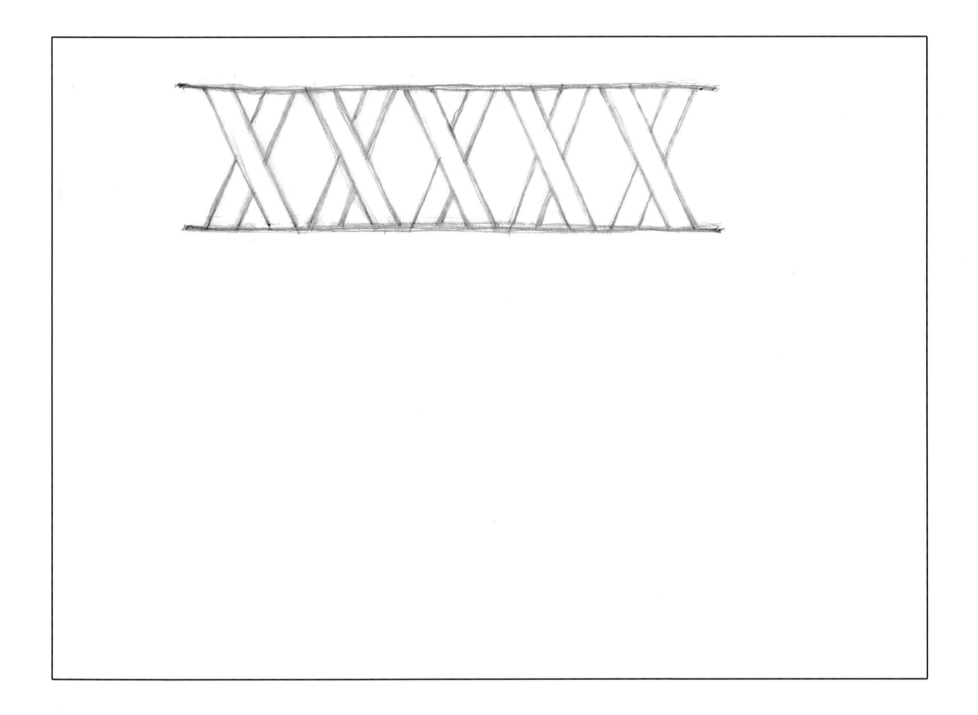

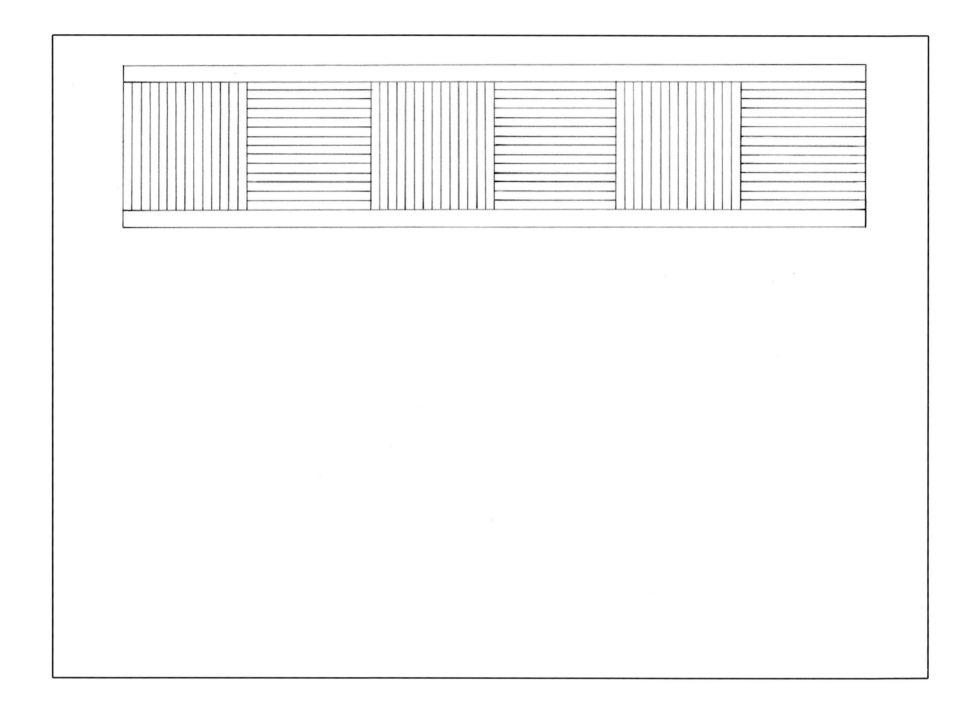

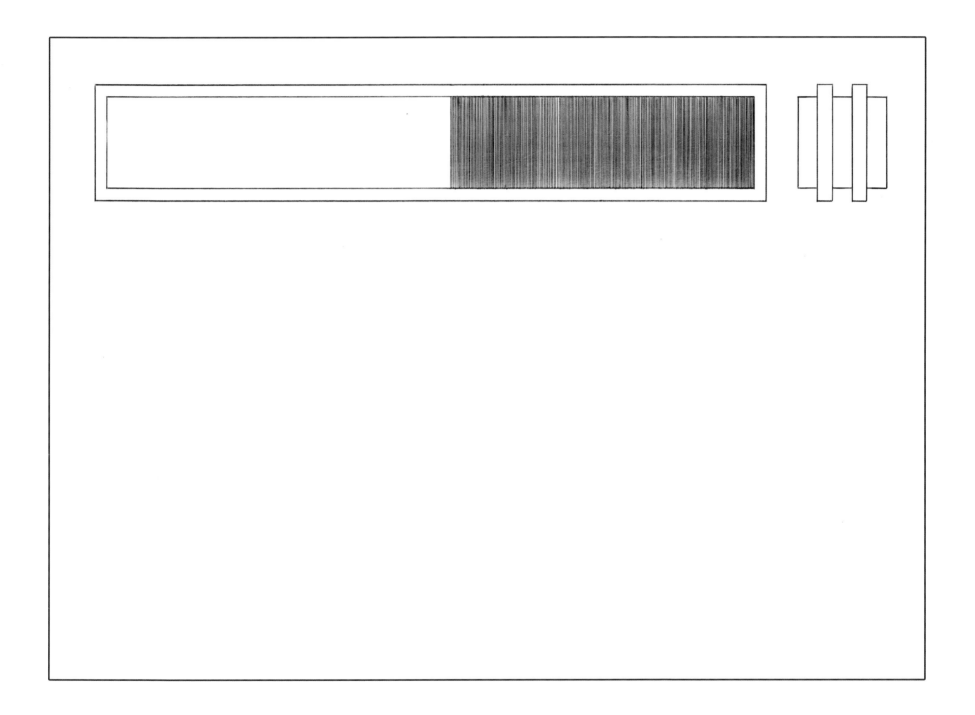

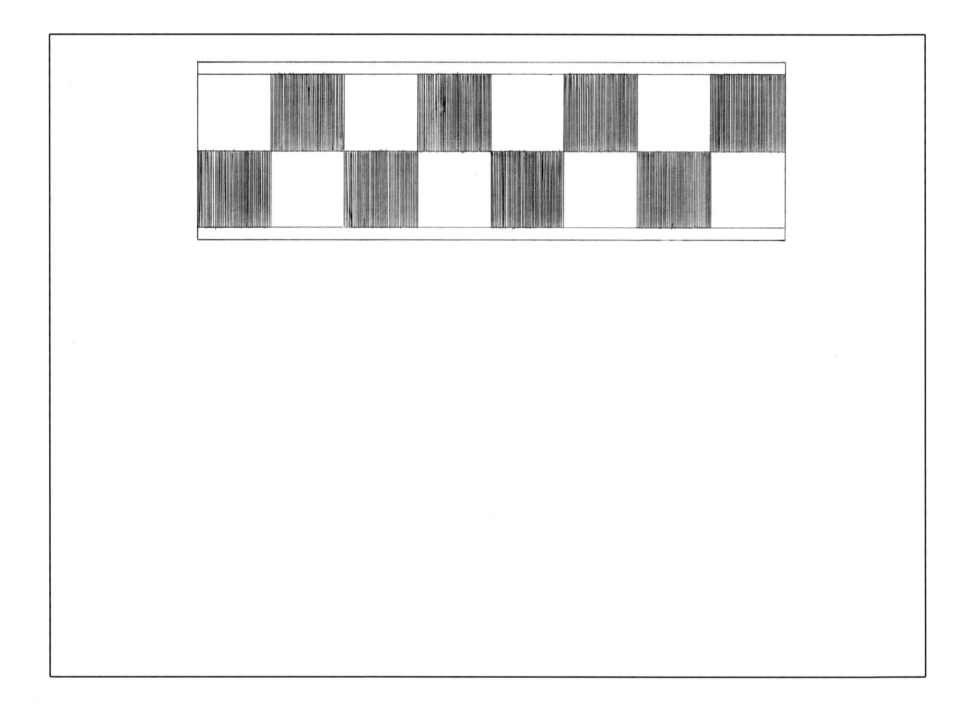

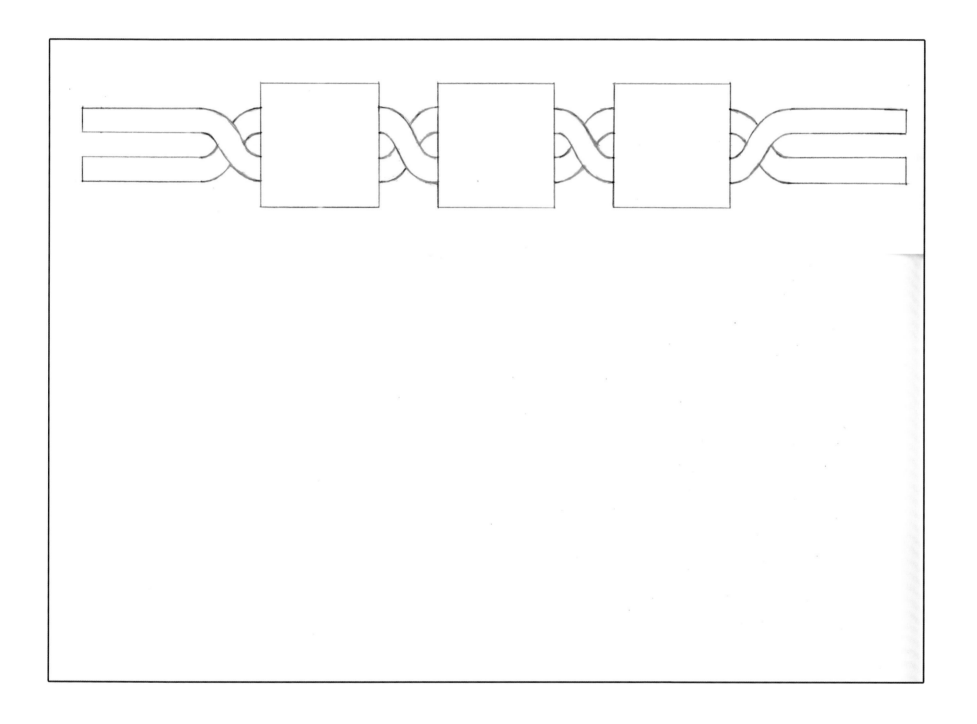

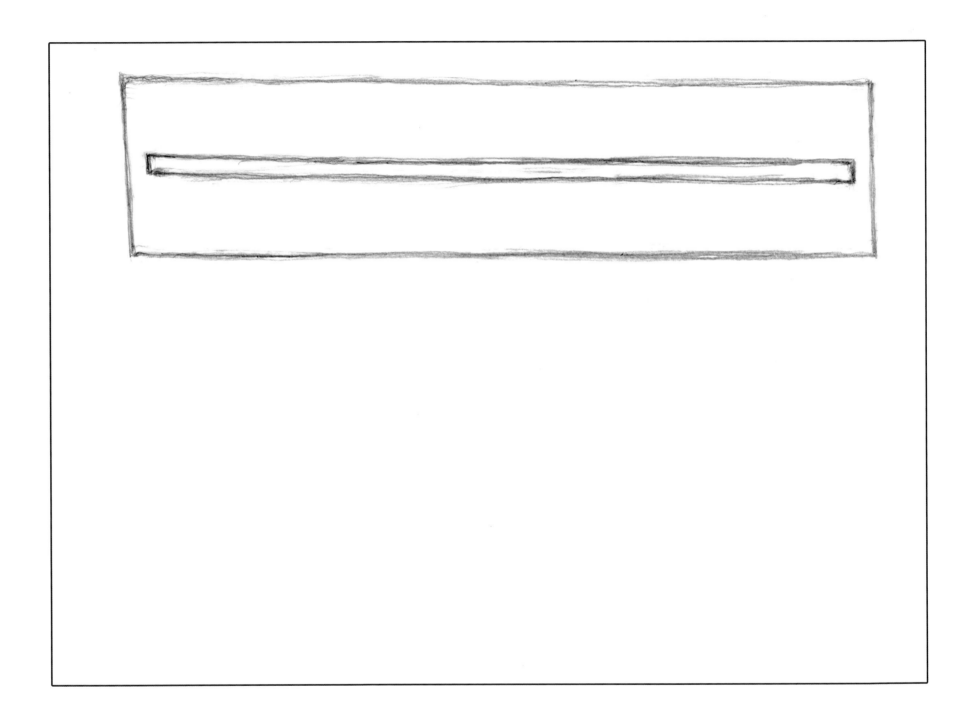

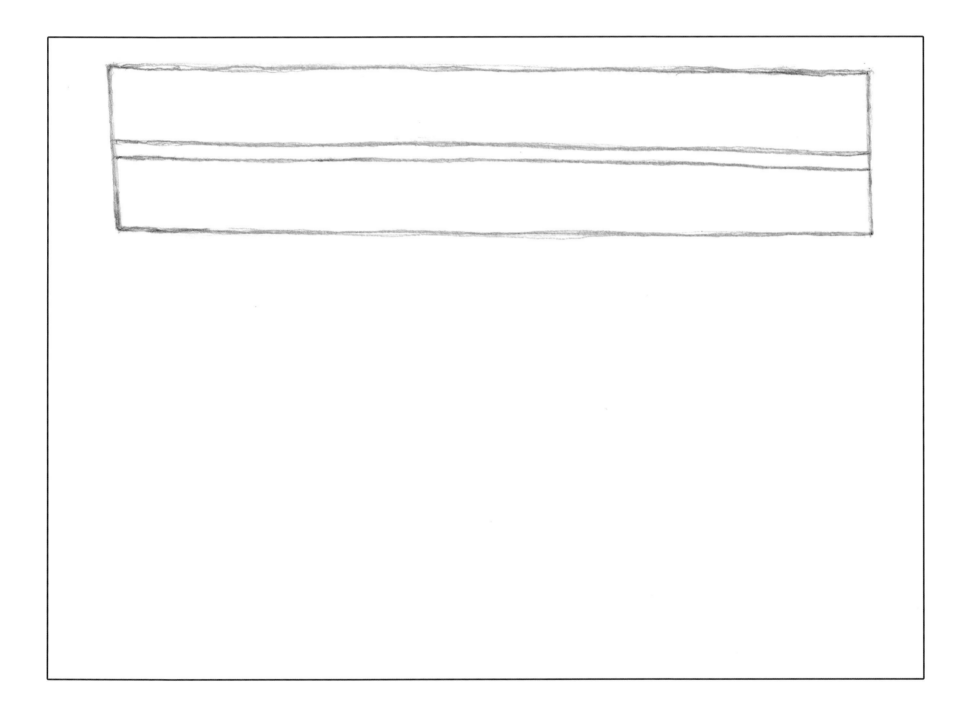

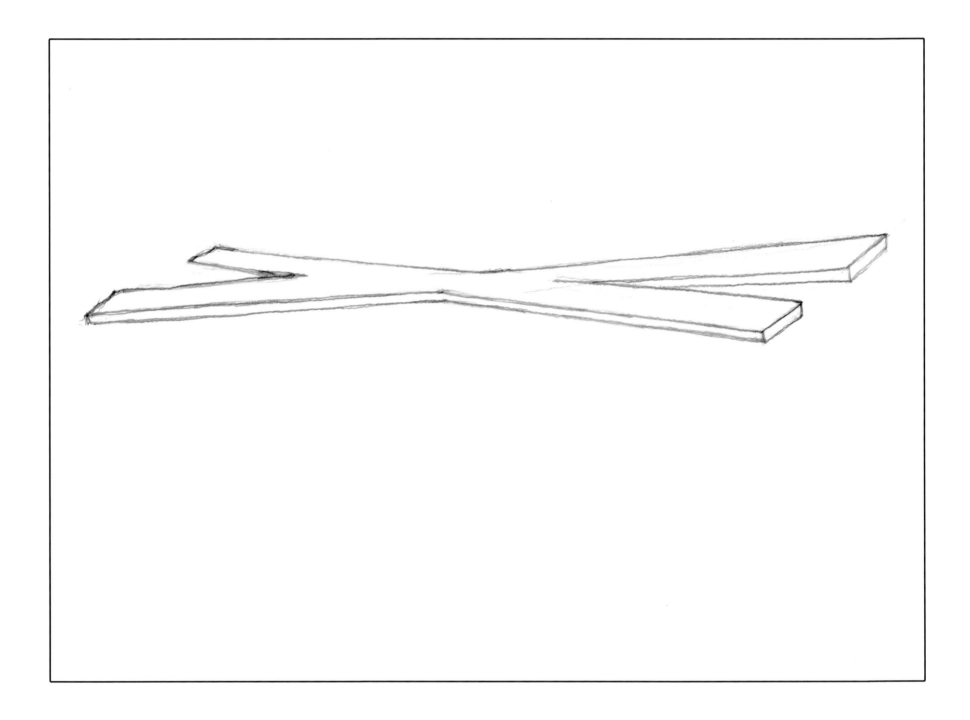

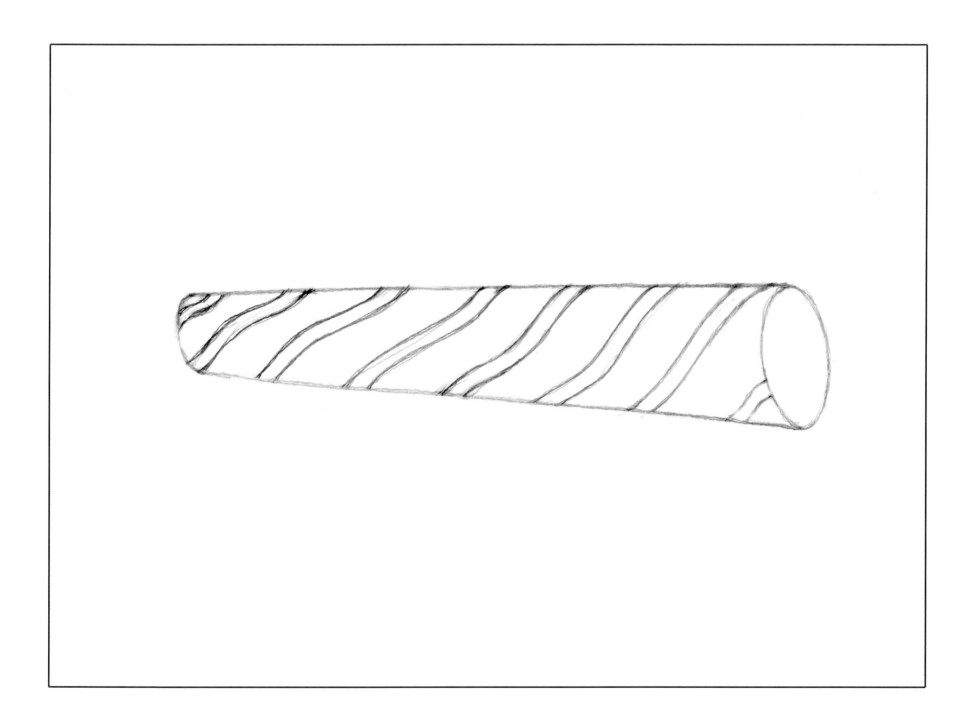

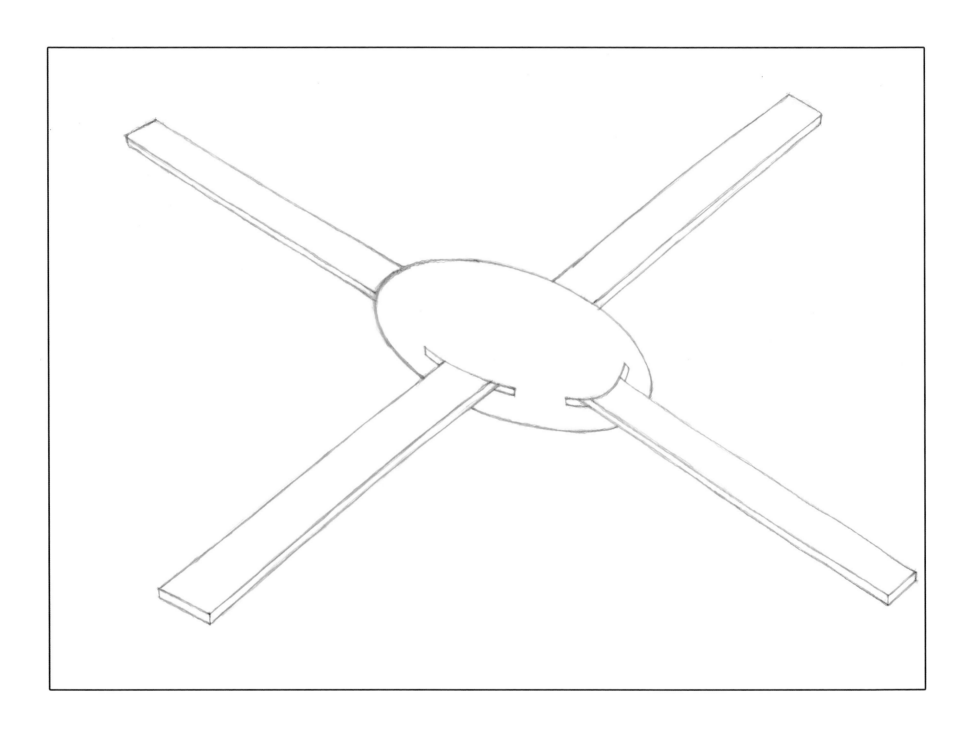

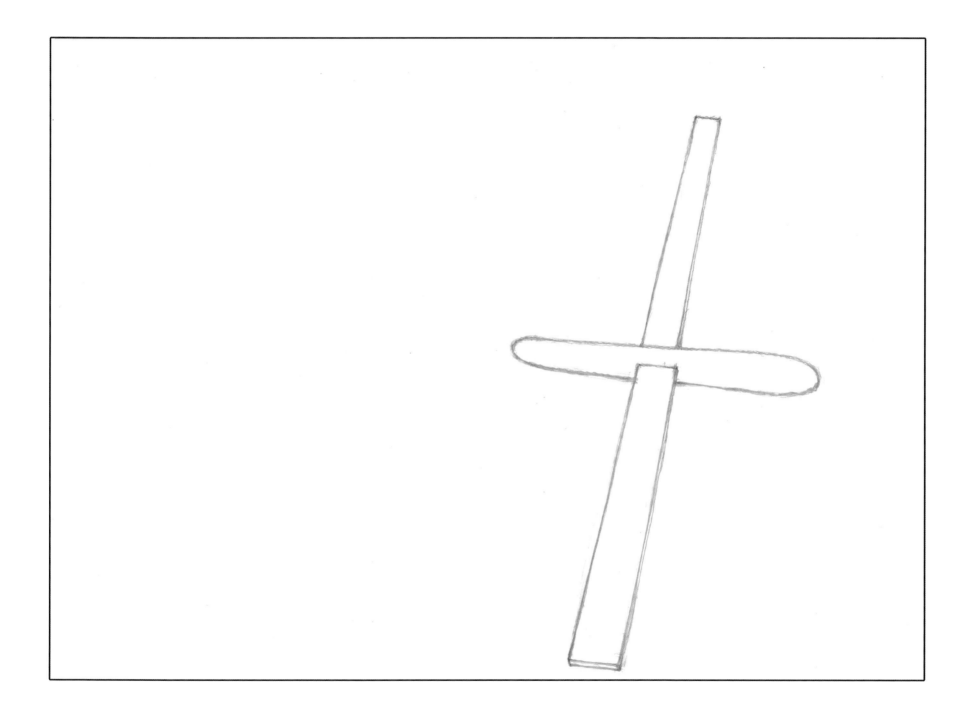

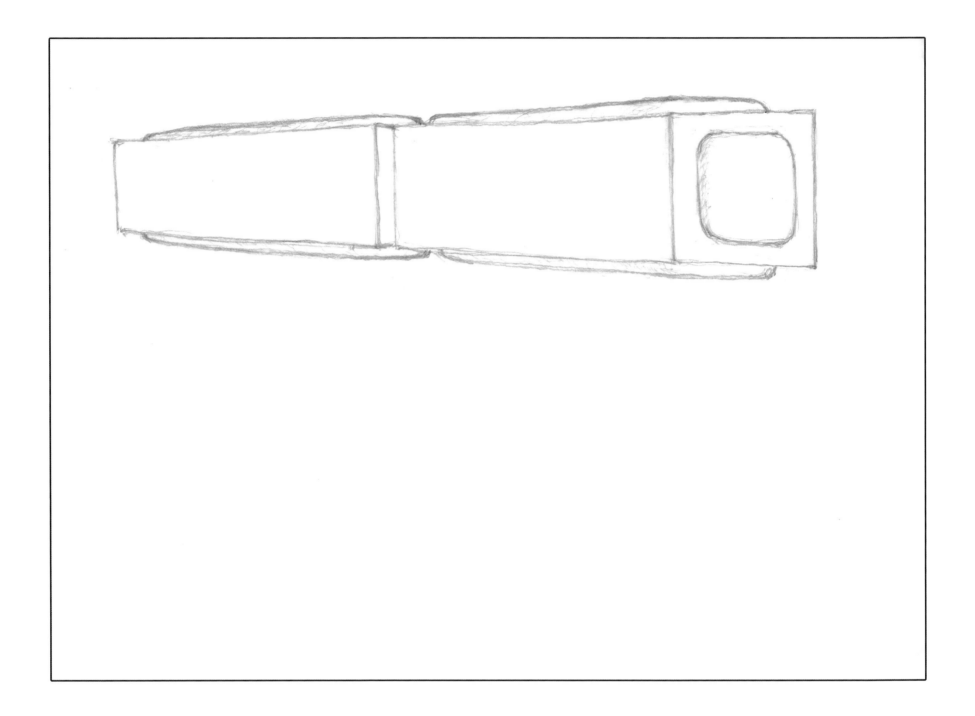

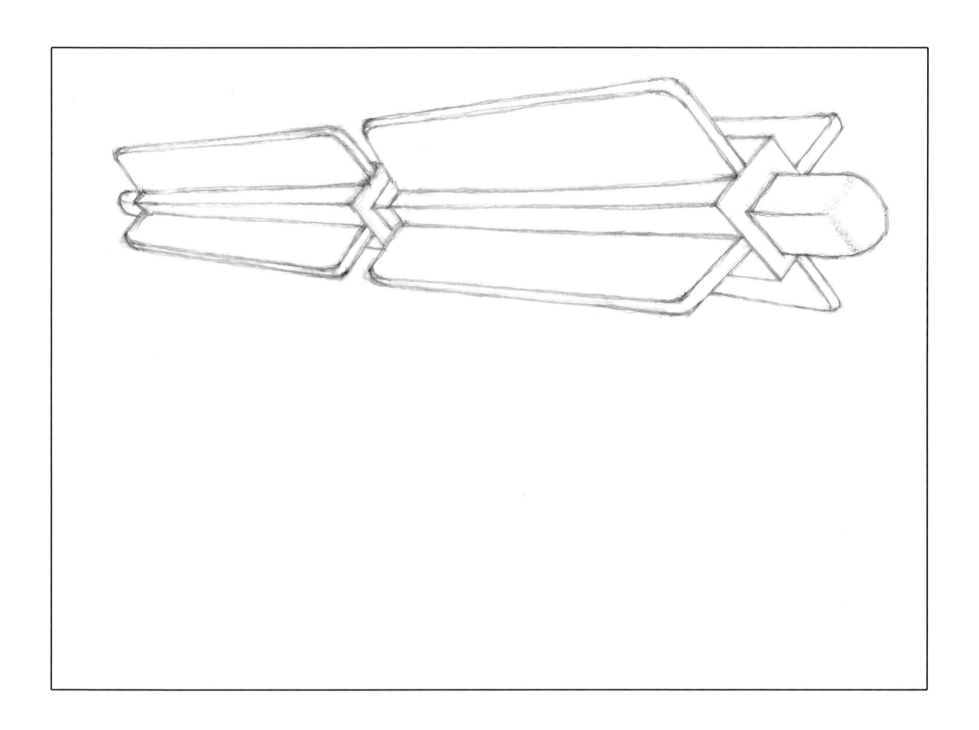

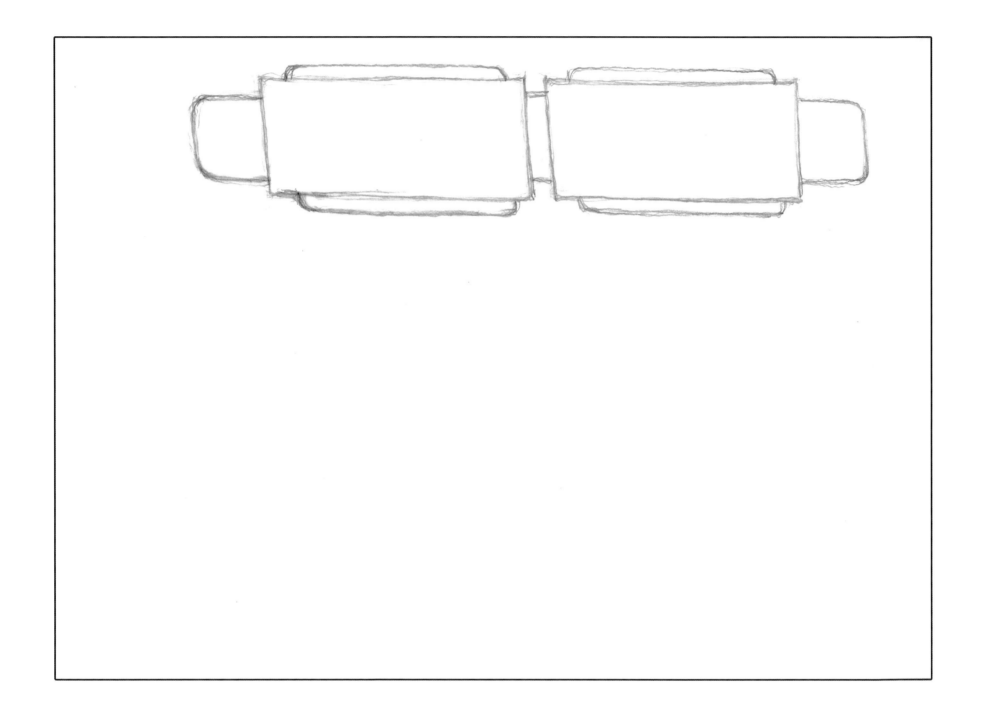

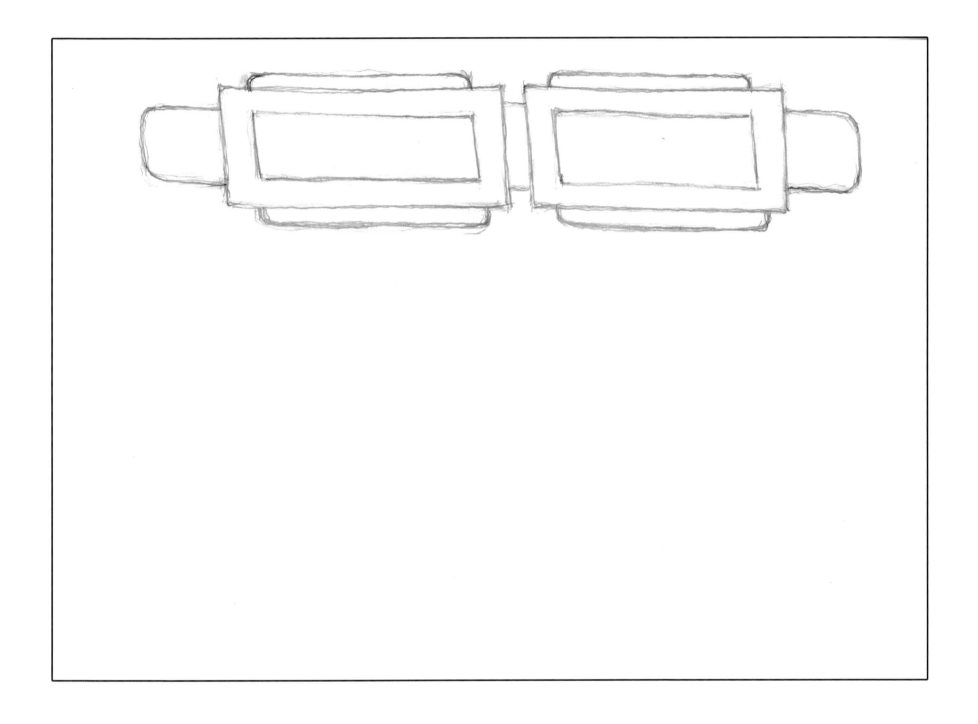

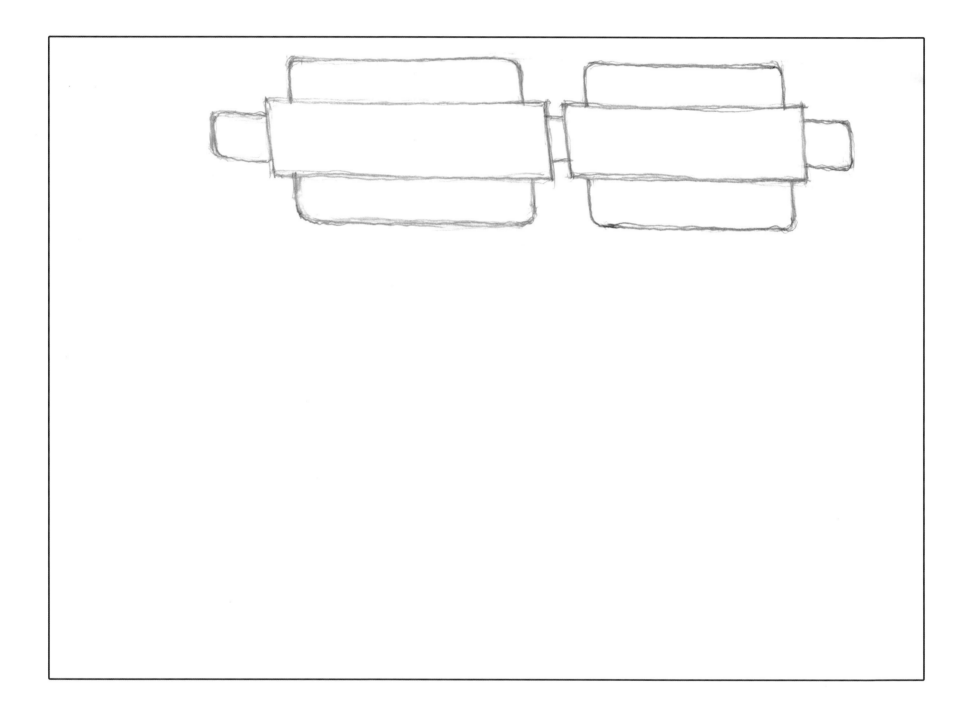

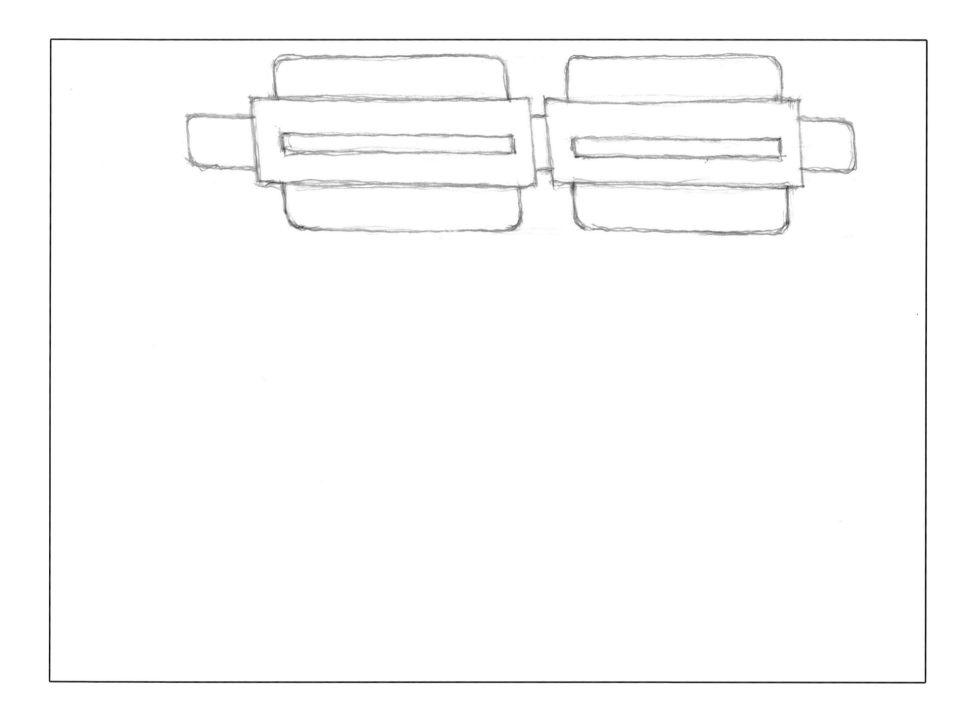

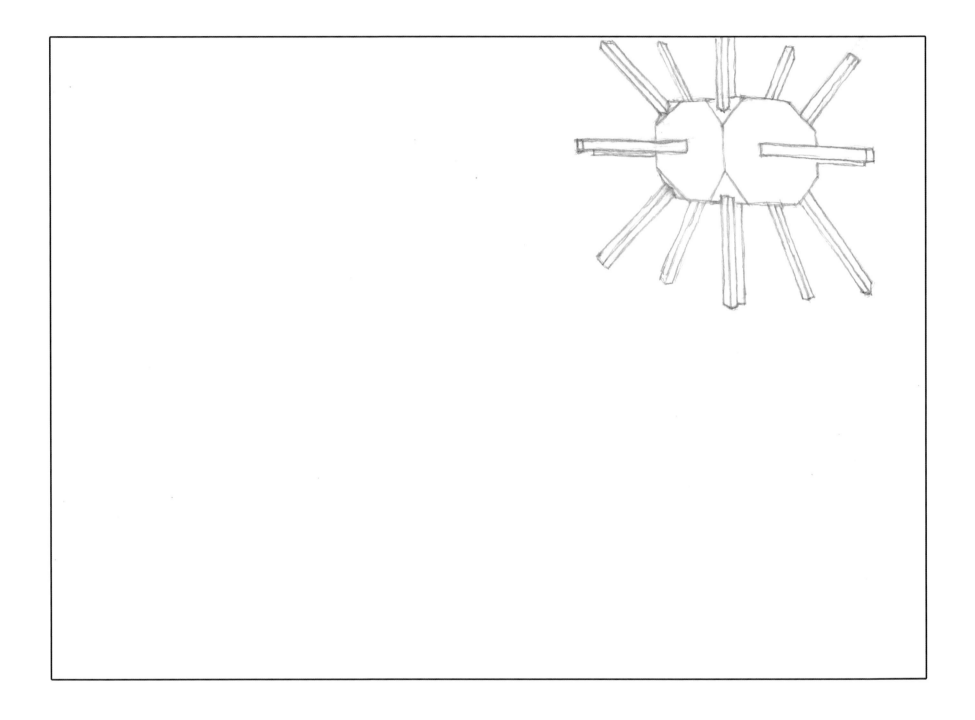

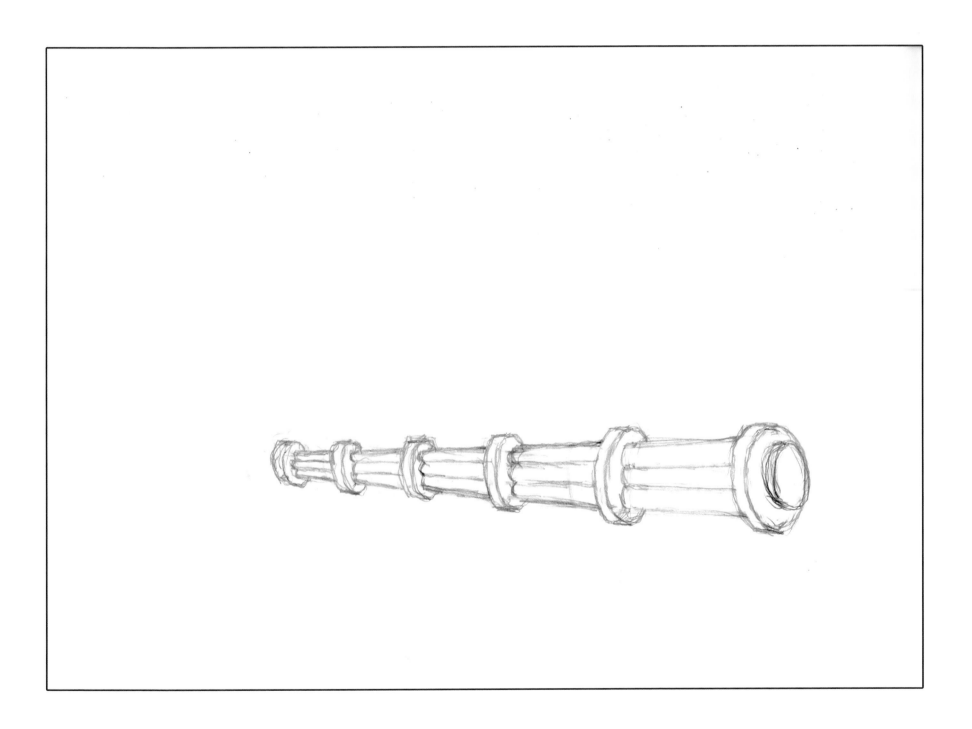

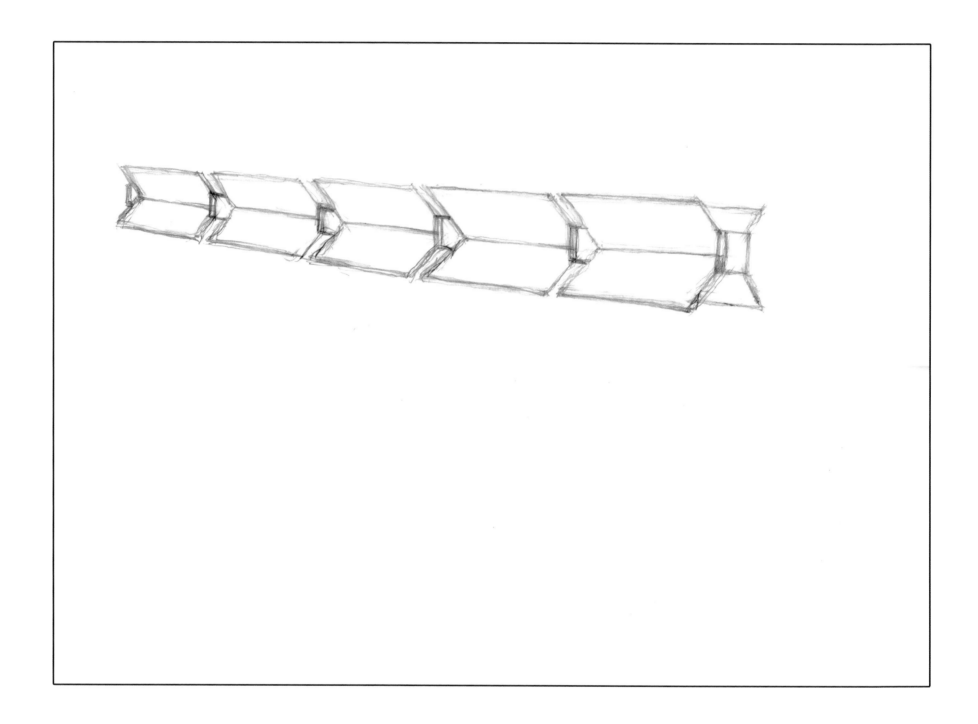

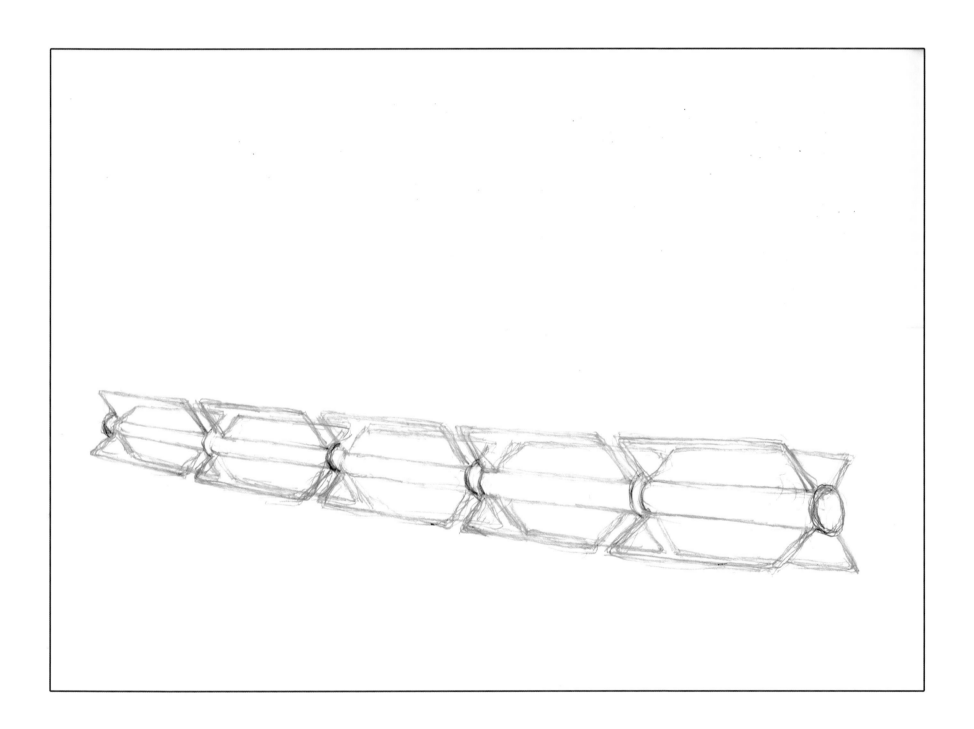

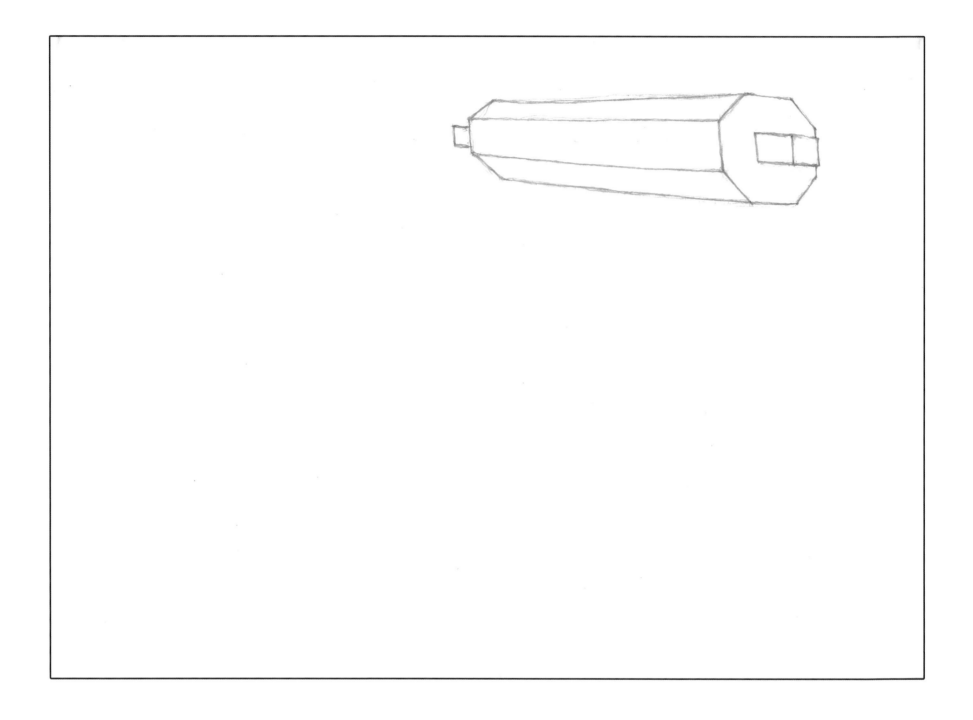

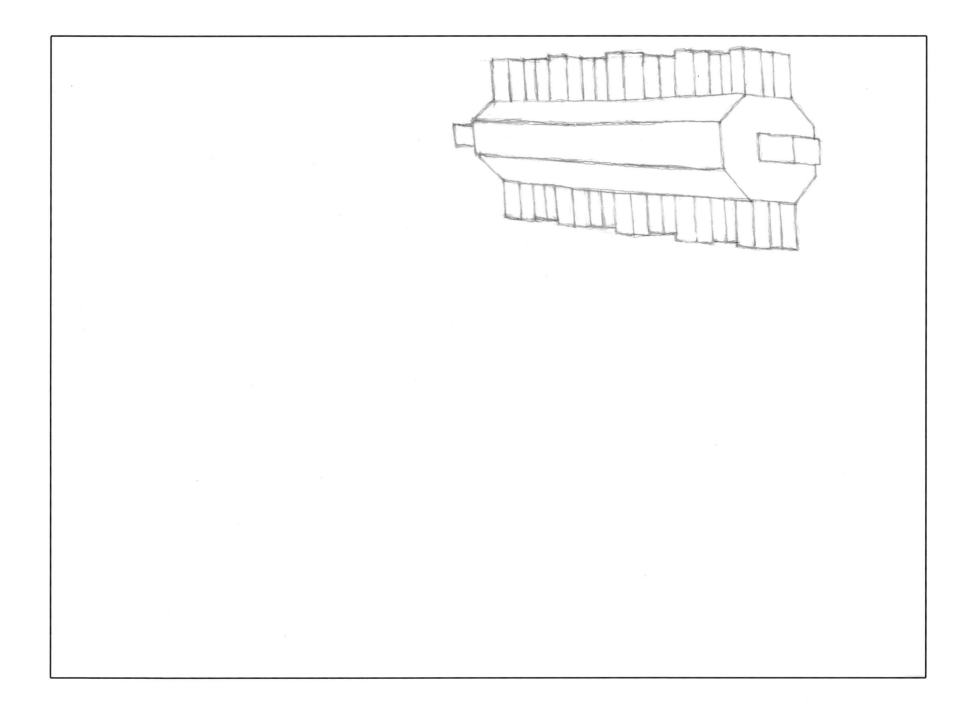

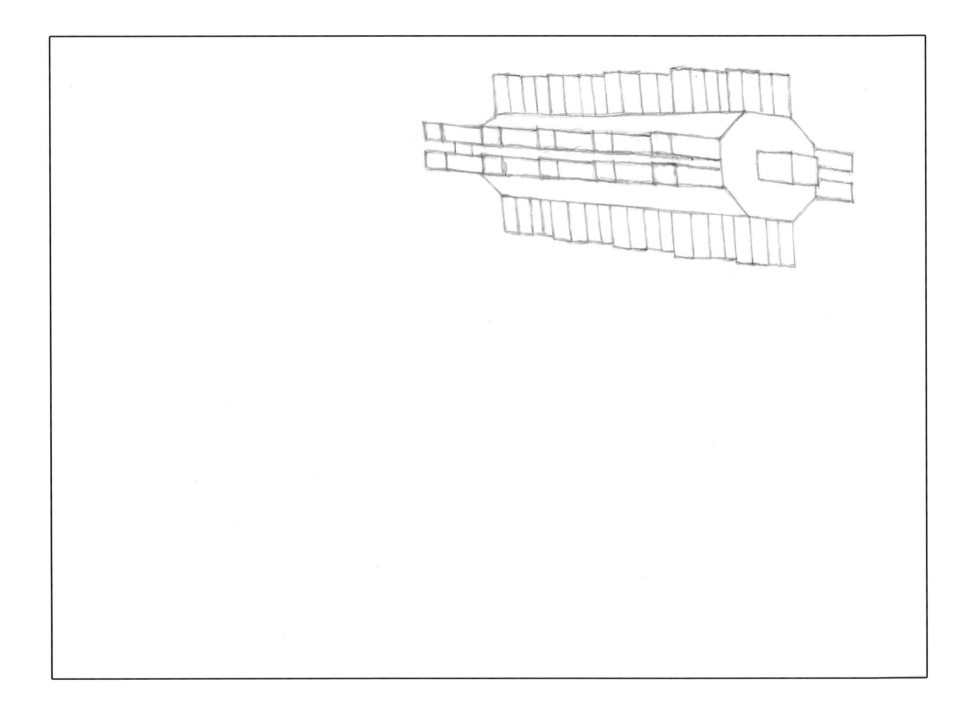

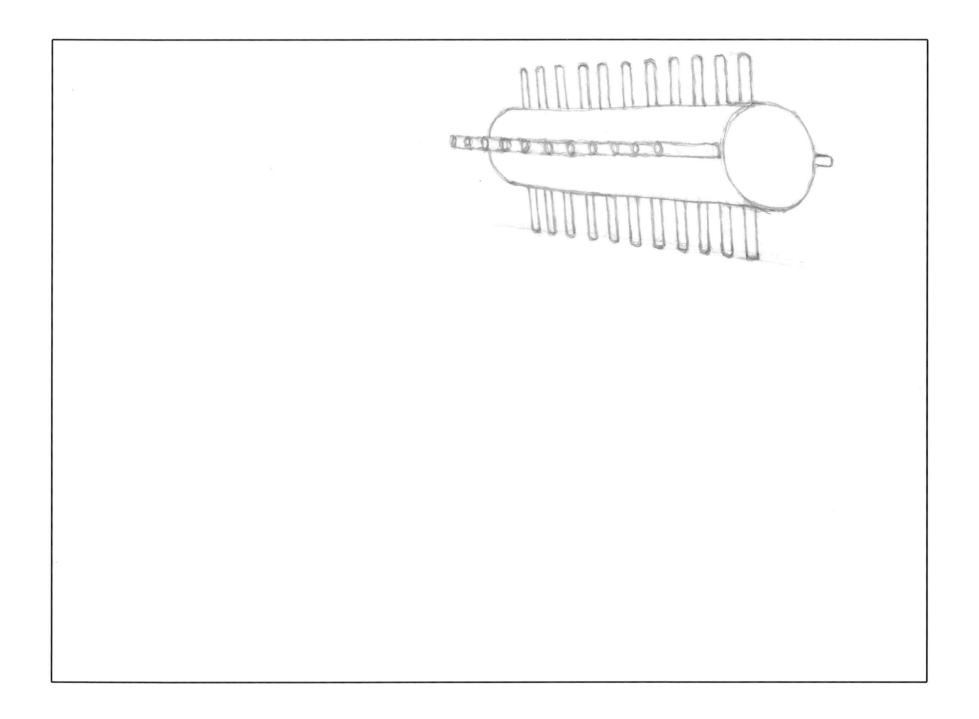

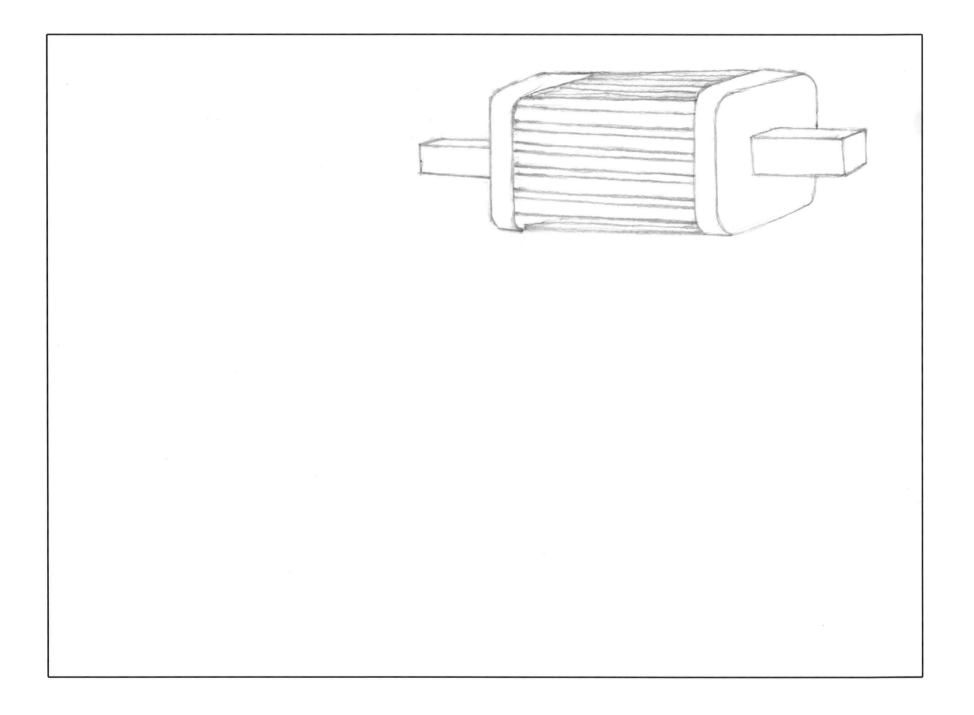

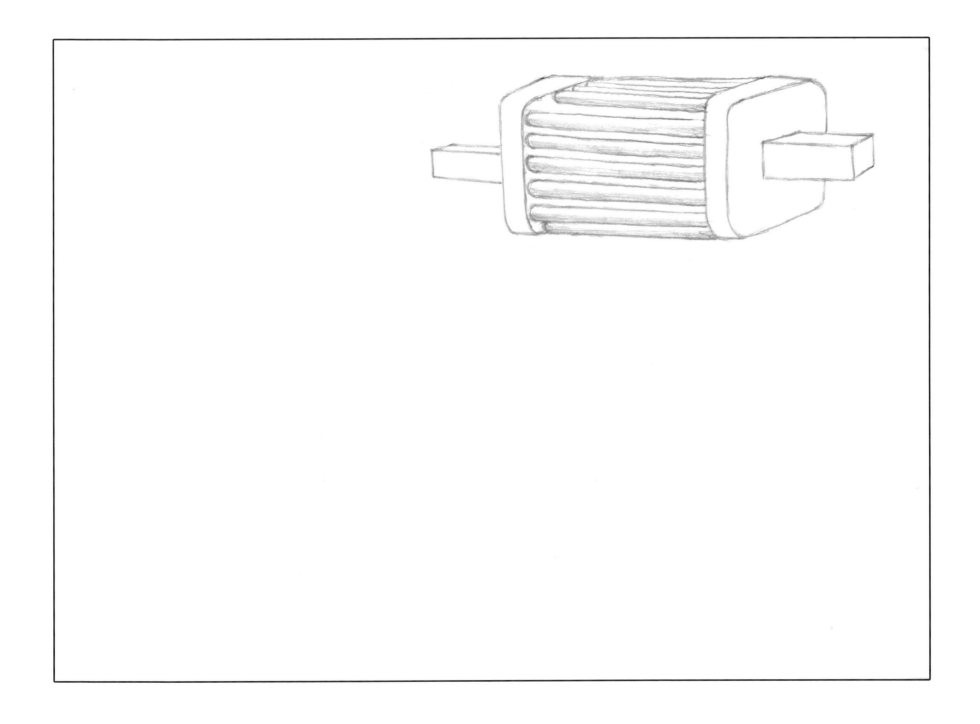

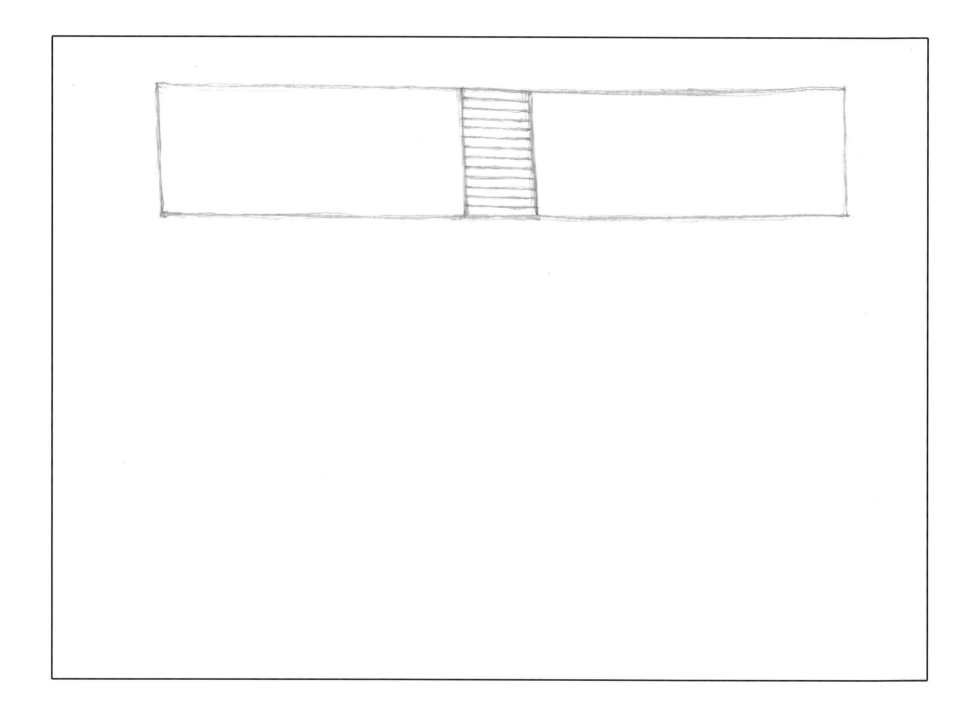

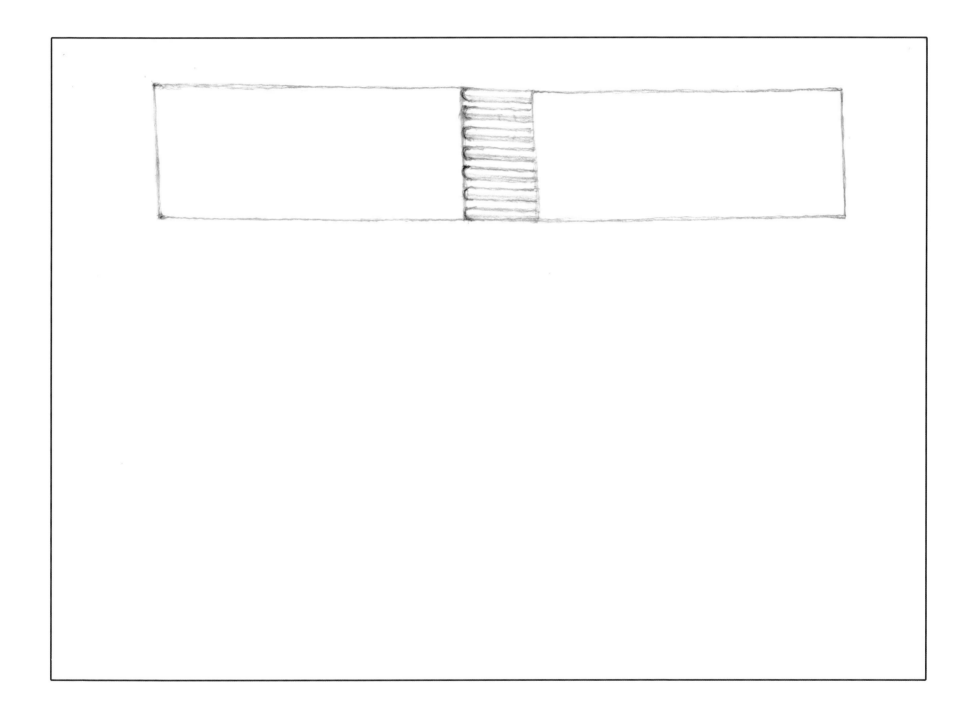

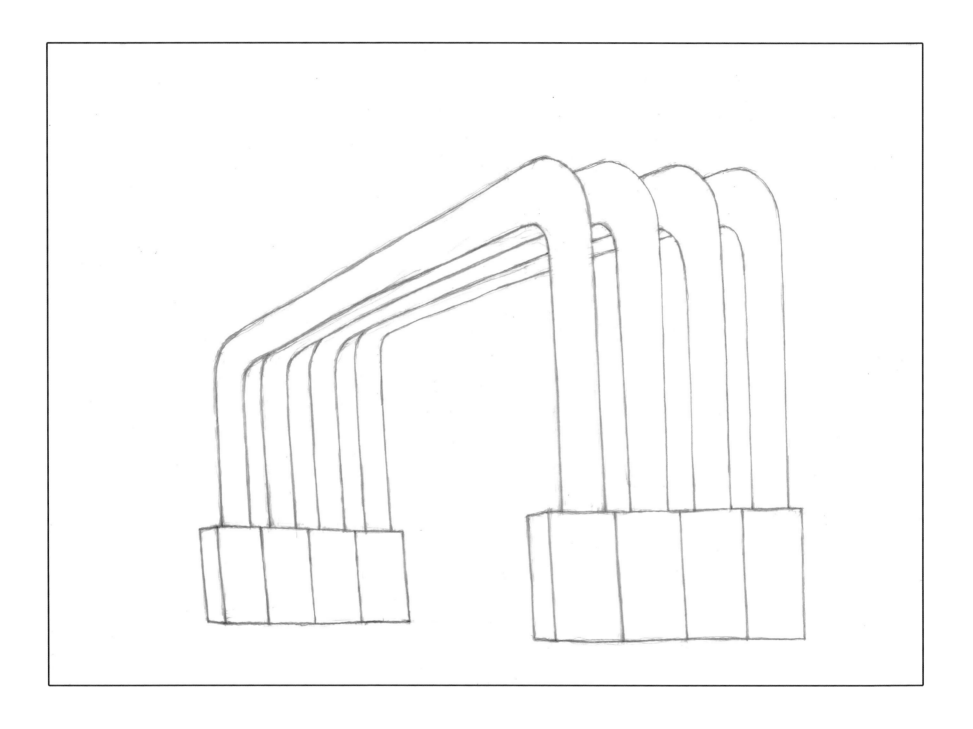

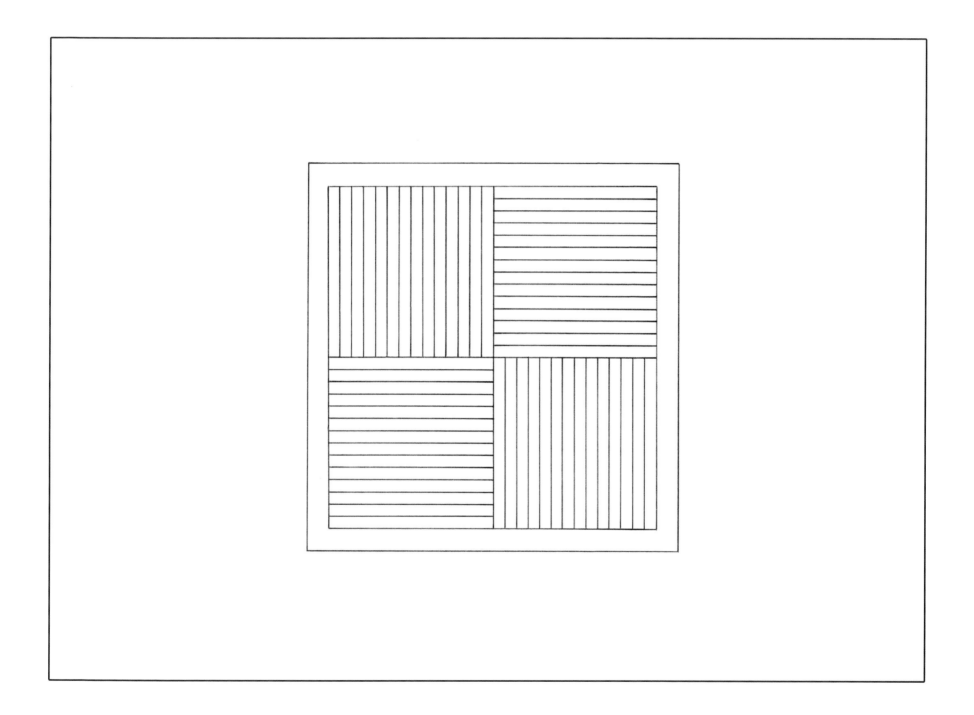

155

List of Works

Sculpture

p. 6-7
Sculpture I
2019
anodized aluminum
6 x 23.2 x 6 cm / 2.36 x 9.13 x 2.36 in.

p. 8-9
Sculpture II
2019
aluminum bake-coated with acrylic resin
6 x 40.7 x 6.5 cm / 2.36 x 16.02 x 2.56 in.

p. 10-11
Sculpture III
2019
anodized aluminum
6 x 44 x 6 cm / 2.36 x 17.32 x 2.36 in.

p. 12-13
Sculpture IV
2019
aluminum bake-coated with acrylic resin
6 x 40.7 x 6.5 cm / 2.36 x 16.02 x 2.56 in.

p. 15
Sculpture V
2018
aluminum bake-coated with acrylic resin
6 x 50 x 6 cm / 2.36 x 19.69 x 2.36 in.

p. 16
Sculpture VI
2018
aluminum bake-coated with acrylic resin
6 x 27.2 x 27.2 cm / 2.36 x 10.7 x 10.7 in.

p. 17
Sculpture V

p. 19
Sculpture VII
2018
aluminum bake-coated with acrylic resin
13.7 x 25 x 12 cm / 5.39 x 9.84 x 4.72 in.

p. 21
Sculpture VII

p. 23
Sculpture VIII
2018
aluminum bake-coated with acrylic resin
6.5 x 47.8 x 6.5 cm / 2.56 x 18.82 x 2.56 in.

p. 25
Sculpture VIII

p. 27
Sculpture IX（Ring Ring Ring）
2018
aluminum
7.5 x 27 x 4.5 cm / 2.95 x 10.63 x 1.77 in.

p. 29
Sculpture IX（Ring Ring Ring）

p. 30-31
Sculpture X（The Bridge）
2018
painted aluminum
7.4 x 38.2 x 4.7 cm / 2.91 x 15.04 x 1.85 in.

p. 33
Sculpture X（The Bridge）

p. 34
Sculpture XI
2018
aluminum, painted white
15 x 16.6 x 16.6 cm / 5.91 x 6.54 x 6.54 in.

p. 35
Sculpture XII
2018
aluminum, painted black
24.2 x 11.6 x 0.3 cm / 9.53 x 4.57 x 0.12 in.

p. 36-37
Sculpture XIII
2018
aluminum, foamed polyurethane
5 x 45 x 5 cm / 1.97 x 17.72 x 1.97 in.

p. 38-39
Sculpture XIII

p. 65
Drawing II
2017
pencil on paper
29.7 x 21 cm / 11.7 x 8.27 in.

p. 66
Drawing III
2017
pencil on paper
42 x 29.7 cm / 16.54 x 11.7 in.

p. 67
Drawing IV
2018
pencil on paper
42 x 29.7 cm / 16.54 x 11.7 in.

p. 68
Drawing V
2017
pencil on paper
29.7 x 21 cm / 11.7 x 8.27 in.

p. 69
Drawing VI
2017
pencil on paper
29.7 x 21 cm / 11.7 x 8.27 in.

p. 70
Drawing VII
2018
pencil on paper
29.7 x 21 cm / 11.7 x 8.27 in.

p. 71
Drawing VIII
2018
pencil on paper
29.7 x 21 cm / 11.7 x 8.27 in.

p. 73
Drawing IX
2018
pencil on paper
29.7 x 42 cm / 11.7 x 16.54 in.

p. 74
Drawing X
2018
pencil on paper
29.7 x 21 cm / 11.7 x 8.27 in.

p. 75
Drawing XI
2018
pencil on paper
29.7 x 21 cm / 11.7 x 8.27 in.

p. 76
Drawing XII
2018
pencil on paper
42 x 29.7 cm / 16.54 x 11.7 in.

p. 77
Drawing XIII
2018
pencil on paper
29.7 x 21 cm / 11.7 x 8.27 in.

p. 78
Drawing XIV
2017
pencil on paper
29.7 x 21 cm / 11.7 x 8.27 in.

p. 79
Drawing XV
2017
pencil on paper
29.7 x 21 cm / 11.7 x 8.27 in.

p. 80
Drawing XVI
2017
pencil on paper
29.7 x 21 cm / 11.7 x 8.27 in.

p. 81
Drawing XVII
2017
pencil on paper
29.7 x 21 cm / 11.7 x 8.27 in.

p. 82
Drawing XVIII
2017
pencil on paper
29.7 x 21 cm / 11.7 x 8.27 in.

p. 83
Drawing XIX
2017
pencil on paper
29.7 x 21 cm / 11.7 x 8.27 in.

p. 84
Drawing XX
2017
pencil on paper
29.7 x 21 cm / 11.7 x 8.27 in.

p. 85
Drawing XXI
2017
pencil on paper
29.7 x 21 cm / 11.7 x 8.27 in.

p. 86
Drawing XXII
2017
pencil on paper
29.7 x 21 cm / 11.7 x 8.27 in.

p. 108
Drawing XLIV
2018
pencil on paper
29.7 x 21 cm / 11.7 x 8.27 in.

p. 109
Drawing XLV
2018
pencil on paper
29.7 x 21 cm / 11.7 x 8.27 in.

p. 110
Drawing XLVI
2018
pencil on paper
29.7 x 21 cm / 11.7 x 8.27 in.

p. 111
Drawing XLVII
2018
pencil on paper
29.7 x 21 cm / 11.7 x 8.27 in.

p. 112
Drawing XLVIII
2018
pencil on paper
29.7 x 21 cm / 11.7 x 8.27 in.

p. 113
Drawing XLIX
2018
pencil on paper
29.7 x 21 cm / 11.7 x 8.27 in.

p. 114
Drawing L
2018
pencil on paper
29.7 x 21 cm / 11.7 x 8.27 in.

p. 115
Drawing LI
2018
pencil on paper
29.7 x 21 cm / 11.7 x 8.27 in.

p. 116
Drawing LII
2018
pencil on paper
29.7 x 21 cm / 11.7 x 8.27 in.

p. 117
Drawing LIII
2018
pencil on paper
29.7 x 21 cm / 11.7 x 8.27 in.

p. 118
Drawing LIV
2018
pencil on paper
42 x 29.7 cm / 16.54 x 11.7 in.

p. 119
Drawing LV
2018
pencil on paper
42 x 29.7 cm / 16.54 x 11.7 in.

p. 120
Drawing LVI
2018
pencil on paper
42 x 29.7 cm / 16.54 x 11.7 in.

p. 121
Drawing LVII
2018
pencil on paper
42 x 29.7 cm / 16.54 x 11.7 in.

p. 122
Drawing LVIII
2018
pencil on paper
42 x 29.7 cm / 16.54 x 11.7 in.

p. 123
Drawing LIX
2018
pencil on paper
42 x 29.7 cm / 16.54 x 11.7 in.

p. 124
Drawing LX
2018
pencil on paper
29.7 x 21 cm / 11.7 x 8.27 in.

p. 125
Drawing LXI
2018
pencil on paper
29.7 x 21 cm / 11.7 x 8.27 in.

p. 126
Drawing LXII
2018
pencil on paper
29.7 x 21 cm / 11.7 x 8.27 in.

p. 127
Drawing LXIII
2018
pencil on paper
29.7 x 21 cm / 11.7 x 8.27 in.

p. 128
Drawing LXIV
2018
pencil on paper
29.7 x 21 cm / 11.7 x 8.27 in.

p. 129
Drawing LXV
2017
pencil on paper
29.7 x 21 cm / 11.7 x 8.27 in.

p. 130
Drawing LXVI
2018
pencil on paper
29.7 x 21 cm / 11.7 x 8.27 in.

p. 131
Drawing LXVII
2018
pencil on paper
29.7 x 21 cm / 11.7 x 8.27 in.

p. 132
Drawing LXVIII
2018
pencil on paper
29.7 x 21 cm / 11.7 x 8.27 in.

p. 133
Drawing LXIX
2018
pencil on paper
29.7 x 21 cm / 11.7 x 8.27 in.

p. 134
Drawing LXX
2018
pencil on paper
42 x 29.7 cm / 16.54 x 11.7 in.

p. 135
Drawing LXXI
2018
pencil on paper
42 x 29.7 cm / 16.54 x 11.7 in.

p. 136
Drawing LXXII
2017
pencil on paper
29.7 x 21 cm / 11.7 x 8.27 in.

p. 137
Drawing LXXIII
2017
pencil on paper
29.7 x 21 cm / 11.7 x 8.27 in.

p. 138
Drawing LXXIV
2017
pencil on paper
29.7 x 21 cm / 11.7 x 8.27 in.

p. 139
Drawing LXXV
2017
pencil on paper
29.7 x 21 cm / 11.7 x 8.27 in.

p. 140
Drawing LXXVI
2017
pencil on paper
29.7 x 21 cm / 11.7 x 8.27 in.

p. 141
Drawing LXXVII
2017
pencil on paper
29.7 x 21 cm / 11.7 x 8.27 in.

p. 142
Drawing LXXVIII
2018
pencil on paper
29.7 x 21 cm / 11.7 x 8.27 in.

p. 143
Drawing LXXIX
2017
pencil on paper
29.7 x 21 cm / 11.7 x 8.27 in.

p. 144
Drawing LXXX
2017
pencil on paper
29.7 x 21 cm / 11.7 x 8.27 in.

p. 145
Drawing LXXXI
2017
pencil on paper
29.7 x 21 cm / 11.7 x 8.27 in.

p. 146
Drawing LXXXII
2018
pencil on paper
29.7 x 21 cm / 11.7 x 8.27 in.

p. 147
Drawing LXXXIII
2018
pencil on paper
29.7 x 21 cm / 11.7 x 8.27 in.

p. 148
Drawing LXXXIV
2018
pencil on paper
29.7 x 21 cm / 11.7 x 8.27 in.

p. 149
Drawing LXXXV
2018
pencil on paper
29.7 x 21 cm / 11.7 x 8.27 in.

p. 150
Drawing LXXXVI
2018
pencil on paper
29.7 x 21 cm / 11.7 x 8.27 in.

p. 151
Drawing LXXXVII
2018
pencil on paper
29.7 x 21 cm / 11.7 x 8.27 in.

p. 152
Drawing LXXXVIII
2018
pencil on paper
29.7 x 21 cm / 11.7 x 8.27 in.

p. 153
Drawing LXXXIX
2018
pencil on paper
29.7 x 21 cm / 11.7 x 8.27 in.

p. 154
Drawing XC
2018
pencil on paper
42 x 29.7 cm / 16.54 x 11.7 in.

p. 155
Drawing XCI
2018
pencil on paper
29.7 x 21 cm / 11.7 x 8.27 in.

Short Essay

About My Sculptures

I make paintings and drawings in a normal fashion, but for sculptures I create scaled-down sculptures or models, capture them in photographs so that they seem their preconceived size, and reproduce them in a book. I endeavor to evoke the same kind of sculptural emotion that would be experienced when actually looking at the sculpture, or an even stronger emotion.
My sculptures are comprised of, and realized through, photographs in my artbooks.

In reality, sculptures tend to be large and present difficulties such as installation sites and storage locations. They are also extremely expensive to create.
Therefore, the creation of sculptures is more difficult than other forms of art, such as paintings.

In contrast to the conventional method that focuses on the actual pieces, I realize them through photographs, which has major advantages.

With sculpture-photographs, it is possible to quickly transform something imagined into scaled-down sculptures and create many sculptures within a short span of time. They also allow me to choose a location or environment in which the sculpture can be installed freely. For example, I can simply compose images of the sculpture and background if I want it to install it in the open air. This makes it possible to install sculptures anywhere in the world.

Sculpture-photographs release me from the restrictions attached to the actual pieces, and allow me to concentrate on the creation of the sculptures themselves.

I reproduce captured images so that they seem to be their preconceived size, which means that many of these scaled-down sculptures captured in photographs can be scaled up to their actual size.

As you can see, this method that I adopt for my sculptures from the perspective of appreciating them from the pages of books allows me to realize the sculptures that they should appear exactly the same as the actual pieces (in the form of books in most cases). In the movie and video communities, a special photographic technique which makes the images feel real is already widely used.

I believe that this new sculpture method has the potential to become an important means of expression in the future.

Eizo Nishio, November 2018

Brief history of the artist

Eizo Nishio: b.1953, Tokyo. / Graduated from the Faculty of Economics, Sophia University, Tokyo, and studied Social Sciences at Waseda University, Tokyo. / Exhibited at Textile as Sculpture, 12th International Biennial of Tapestry at Cantonal Museum of Fine Arts, Lausanne, Switzerland, 1985, and KUNSTEN - Museum of Modern Art Aalborg, Denmark, 1985. / Established Art & Books in Tokyo, 1987. / Writes articles and comments for all periodicals published by Art & Books. / Published **20/21C ART BOOKS**, 2010, **Eizo Nishio: Sculptures & Drawings 2011-2014**, 2014, **Eizo Nishio: Paintings. Square and Long Rectangle**, 2015, and other books.

Editing by Eizo Nishio
Photographs by Eizo Nishio

ISBN 978-4-909594-10-5

Art & Books Publishers, Tokyo
www.artbibliography.com